How To Play HARMONICA
...instantly

by Marcos

Published by

HARP'N Music Publishing Company

ACKNOWLEDGMENTS

History portion and photographs are courtesy of Hohner Harmonicas.

I would like to dedicate this book to my loved ones, associates and friends.

TABLE OF CONTENTS

ABOUT THE AUTHOR

Nashville 1976 D.J. Convention.

ABOUT THE AUTHOR

Out of perhaps millions of harmonica lovers the world over, only a dozen or so are recognized virtuosos. Marcos is, and has been for over ten years, a recognized virtuoso on harmonica. His musical performances have made it into every possible music-media form—records, film scores, television, performing with superstars of all types of music. Virtuoso says it all!

He attended UCLA on a scholarship for Film Scoring and Orchestration. He is sought after by many harmonica lovers and students for instruction on his insights and techniques. Whether you know it or not, you've probably heard him playing harmonica at one time or another, and you will again. He wrote this book for harmonica lovers everywhere to share the simple beauty of his unique methods for learning to play harmonica with his own self-styled expertise.

I applaud this book and the fine musician who wrote it. I highly recommend it to all levels of harmonica players.

Barry R. Brownlee
TV Producer, Award winning writer

PLAY TODAY

You will be playing songs you know and love by the time you've finished the first small section of this book. Even if you can't read music and have never played a musical instrument, you'll find the easy steps will make you a musician almost immediately. The first section is called GETTING THE FEEL, and it is designed to make it easy for you to play real music out of your harmonica. In no time you'll become intimately familiar with your "harp," and tunes will never be elusive again! You will love it.

Those of you who are among the more advanced harmonica players may skip the first section and get to the meatier second section, GETTING GOOD. Devoted to simplicity and ease, this section reveals the tricks and techniques of the pros. Even the exercises are made simple and fun, but they are specifically designed to instill genuine skill with minimal time and effort.

The extra sections contain vintage photos showing the evolution of the harmonica—courtesy of the main source and development of this precision instrument, Hohner. Charts on models available are included along with many easy to follow illustrations. Vital tips on the care and maintenance of the harmonica are also included in the back of the book. And you'll find lots of great songs throughout.

Anyone can learn to play harmonica!

GETTING

INSIGHT

The history of the harmonica is a love story as ancient as music and as contemporary as today. In this section you'll find vintage photographs to go along with the chronological history of the harmonica.

Some important tips on the construction, care, and maintenance round out the section, which includes a photographic breakdown as well as more illustrations. You'll want to keep this section for reference through your years of making sweet music on the harmonica.

Hohner's first advertising poster.

HARMONICA HISTORY

Many of us, when we first think of a harmonica, tend to visualize a lone cowboy, leg hooked over his saddle horn as he rides along playing a tune to amuse himself and help keep the cattle from growing restless during a long night on the open range. Or, perhaps, we see the famous *Harmonicats* tapping to the beat while they play their well known rendition of "Peg o' My Heart."

But there is far more to the history and versatility of the harmonica than that. It is an instrument loved and played throughout the world by millions of people in a variety of styles ranging from classical to rock to country, blues, jazz and polkas.

The harmonica's history can be traced back to China in 3000 B.C., when Emperor Nyn-Kwa is believed to have created a free swinging reed instrument known as the "Sheng." Marco-Polo is credited with introducing this bowl-shaped instrument throughout Europe in the 18th century. In Europe, the harmonica became the forerunner of the reed organ, the accordion, the saxophone and the harmonica.

The "Sheng"

The Sheng is made from bamboo reeds that vibrate freely when air is blown into it.

The harmonica began to take on its shape and distinctiveness as we know it today when in 1821, a German clockmaker by the name of Christian Friedrich Ludwig Buschmann, put 15 pitch pipes together to form a square instrument four inches on a side. Buschmann's 21-note instrument, which he called the "mundaeoline" (a German word meaning mouth) had the versatility of piano and cresendo without piano keys.

Soon another clockmaker, Christian Messner, learned how to make Buschmann's little instrument and developed a profitable sideline selling his harmonicas to other clockmakers.

Vintage Harmonicas

Round openings with lead plates
One of the first harmonicas made (1885).

Hand carved ivory harmonica (1885).

One of the first made Trossinger harmonicas (1830)
called the "Old Christian Witness."

7 Ocatave lead plate harmonica (1830).
wood whittled with a knife.

The Hohner Factory in 1857

Matthias Hohner 1833 - 1902

However, it was not until 1857 that harmonicas began ot be available on a regular basis. That was when 24 year old Matthias Hohner decided that harmonicas could be produced in larger numbers using factory methods. Hohner opened a small factory in Trossingen, Germany where in his first year of business he, along with his wife and two employees, made 650 harmonicas. There was a growing market for his harmonicas in Europe, but after his cousin immigrated to New York taking a few of the instruments with him, a large portion of Hohner's sales came from the United States.

Matthias Hohner's original tools.

In America, during the Civil War, the harmonica became an even more popular and well known instrument. It was small and durable, which made it possible for soldiers to carry it with them wherever they went. Also, since it was easy to learn how to play, soldiers from both the North and South increasingly found comfort and pleasure in the melodies and sometimes haunting sound of the harmonicas.

After the war the harmonica continued to grow in popularity, crossing both geographic and economic barriers with ease. As Americans moved west they took harmonicas with them. Because of its shirt pocket size and unique sound the harmonica was popular with the troops patrolling the vast, lonely frontiers and with the pioneers moving slowly but steadily westward to fill that space.

Trumpet Call Harmonica—with
five amplifying horns

Harmonette, piano shaped
Harmonica with sound hole—1930's

Glockenspiel Harmonica
with bells

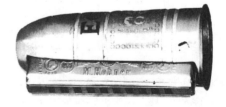

Echophone Harmonica—
Brass cone for amplification

In the south the black farmers, facing new frontiers of their own, found the harmonica a better instrument than their own "quills," which were homemade instruments made of varying lengths of cane strapped together. They were inventive with the harmonica, learning to make new sounds, many of which later became part of the blues sound—their unique and special contribution to the world of music.

At least two American presidents have had a fondness for harmonicas. Legend has it that when Stephen Douglas came to the famous Lincoln–Douglas debates accompanied by a brass band that Abraham Lincoln took out his own harmonica and quipped, "Mr. Douglas needs a brass band but the harmonica will do for me." Although he was more well known for the Tea Pot Dome scandals, Warren G. Harding kept a collection of harmonicas while he was in the White House.

By the late 1920s and early 1930s, with the advent of radio and audio recordings, the harmonica was a well established instrument used by both the white string bands and the black ragtime bands. There were numerous talented musicians, both black and white, in this era who did their part to insure the harmonica a place in musical history.

Among them was Larry Adler, who played pop music, classical musician Eddy Manson, and the lengendary DeFord Bailey, a black man who, despite racial barriers, played on 48 out of the 52 "Grand Ole Opry" broadcasts in 1928.

Then there was Lonnie Glosson whose special skill was his ability to make the harmonica "talk." Perhaps the most famous example of his talent was his recording of "I Want My Momma" made in the 1950s. However, it is Glosson's protege,' Wayne Raney, who is credited with doing more than any other single person in the 20th century to popularize the harmonica. Broadcasting on radio station WCKY in Cincinnati, Ohio, Raney did more than just sing and play the harmonica, he *sold* them as well. It has been said that from 1945 to 1950 Wayne Raney sold an average of a million harmonicas a year by mail order!

However, with the coming of rock music—accompanied by the use of amplification—the popularity of the harmonica faded in the late 1950s and early 1960s (even though it flourished in Chicago's South Side, one of the prominent *blues* holdouts of the nation). But musicians, being the innovative breed they are, continued to experiment with new music forms, and the harmonica proved its versatility once again. They soon learned that, with amplification, the harmonica could hold its own in groups of most any size as well as for solo purposes.

Today the harmonica is a regular part of the rock, pop and blues music, used by such famous artists as Bob Dylan, Neil Young, Julian Lennon, Stevie Wonder, John Mayall, Paul Butterfield, Charlie Musselwhite, Eddy Manson, Sonny Terry, Huie Louis, James Cotton, Junior Wells, and others. The harmonica was instrumental in creating that special country sound being used by Johnny Cash, Charlie McCoy, Wayon Jennings, and a host of others too numerable to list individually.

For sheer size of musical groups, nothing has ever exceeded the 1700 lads in the Boy Scout Harmonica Band which performed at a 1981 *Boy Scout Jamboree* at Fort A. P. Hill, Virginia. This one-time performance—which included the playing of Dixie, America the Beautiful, and Battle Hymn of the Republic—earned a place in the "Guinness Book of World Records" for largest gathering of musicians playing a single instrument in a single performance.

Much has changed in the world of music and in the development of the harmonica, but there is also a great deal that has remained much as it was, especially the leadership and quality production of harmonicas founded by M. Hohner. In addition to still producing harmonicas at its original factory site in Trossingen, Germany, Hohner now has large facilities in Palo Alto, California and Ashland, Virginia.

Although the most popular harmonica made today is the Marine Band model first introduced in 1896, there are over 50 models available ranging in size from 1¼ to 23 inches long. Each of these instruments made at Hohner today gets the same special kind of attention and hand tuning that the first Hohner harmonicas received over 120 years ago.

Many of the people who sit in isolation booths at the factory listening as a fan blows air through the reeds one at a time to be sure that each harmonica has a perfect tone are second- and third-generation tuners. Hohner believes that the skill required for this kind of work runs in some families and he makes every effort to hire them. This is just one example of the many steps that the Hohner Company takes to insure that the instruments produced in their factories meet the high quality standards of the professional and amateur alike.

In spite of all the sources of music available in our modern electronic age through radio, records, television, and video tapes, there is still nothing quite like the satisfaction of being able to create one's "own" music. This, more than any other one thing, may be responsible for the continued popularity of the harmonica. Anyone with the desire to do so can take this small, hand-held instrument and in a short time become a musician capable of playing old familiar tunes and creating new melodies of one's very own.

1. First listen to the cassette tape all the way through.
2. Then go back to the start of the tape to learn and practice. If you are having any problems at any part of the cassette tape, STOP TAPE, REWIND AND PLAY THAT PART AGAIN until you fully understand.
3. As an alternative, you can just play the tape through several times and improve your skill as you go along..

SECTION I

GETTING THE FEEL

BLOW ↑
DRAW ↓

Top set of reeds
are Blow notes;
bottom set of
reeds are Draw
notes

Even if you can only see a single row of holes in your harmonica, it actually has two rows of ten holes for playing. That's because the harmonica is a "sandwich" of two plates of tuned reeds. Air leaving your mouth goes through the reeds on one of the plates, and air entering your mouth comes through the reeds on the other. When you orient the harmonica properly—like a piano, so that low-register notes are produced by the end at the left and high notes at the right—**the top set of reeds is played by air BLOWN** into the holes. **The bottom set of reeds is played with the air DRAWN** through the holes. DRAWING is achieved by actually inhaling, as if drawing a liquid through a straw.

The holes are numbered 1 to 10, and each numbered hole has an UPPER reed (for blowing into) and a LOWER reed (for drawing through). The blowing or drawing determines which notes are played, as each hole plays only one note at a time. In this book, an arrow pointing up or down by a number is the way I tell you which hole to play and whether to BLOW or DRAW. The number is the hole, and the arrow up (↑) means BLOW, arrow down (↓) means DRAW. Whole songs can be played note for note by following the charts of numbered arrows in this book. With very little practice, you'll become familiar with the harmonica notes corresponding to the numbers and arrows. As your familiarity increases, the transitions between notes becomes smooth and easy. When it does, you can consider yourself a musician. For best results, follow these steps for getting the feel:

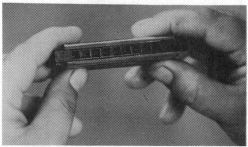

BLOW ↑
DRAW ↓

1. Pick up your harmonica, moisten your lips, and take a deep breath; exhale partially. Take the harmonica between your lips, careful to place your lips onto the metal plates without touching your teeth. Now BLOW and slide the harmonica from side to side without moving your head—playing all ten of the upper row notes back and forth.

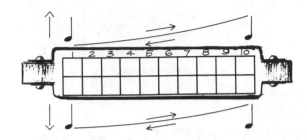

BLOW ↑
DRAW ↓

2. Now DRAW (↓) on the harmonica, sliding it back and forth to play the lower row notes 1 through 10.

3. Moisten your lips whenever necessary, and alternate blowing and drawing over all ten holes. This is a good warmup to get the reeds vibrating, similar to stretching your legs before running.

4. Try to play one individual note (hole 1—the lowest—is generally the easiest). Purse your lips as if to whistle, so the air will be confined to a single hole to produce one pure note.

BLOW ↑
DRAW ↓

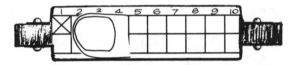

5. Notice that, once in place, your lips can remain to DRAW without any real change. Try blowing and drawing the individual notes of all ten holes several times.

6. Now, being specific, BLOW at hole 1 and DRAW at hole 10. Do this several times for good measure.

7. Reverse now and BLOW at 10 and DRAW at 1. In a few minutes you should be playing all four notes clearly.

BLOW ↑
DRAW ↓

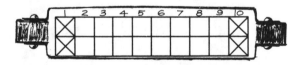

8. Starting at hole 1, slowly BLOW single notes up to hole 10, counting to yourself the hole numbers as you go. Then DRAW 1 to 10 using the same method.

9. The upper-row note on hole 4 is particularly important, because it is the key note that matches the key stamped on the harmonica. If the harmonica is

stamped with the letter C, the upper hole (the BLOW hole) of 4 is C. Upper 1 and 10 are also C, though an octave higher and lower in pitch. Try to BLOW a single clear note on 4. It's all right to look at the numbers before playing, but you'll quickly learn to feel the note with practice—that's a promise!

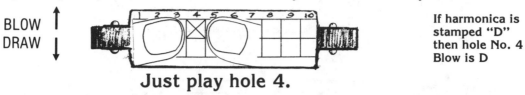

BLOW ↑
DRAW ↓

Just play hole 4.

If harmonica is stamped "D" then hole No. 4 Blow is D

10. Use the tip of your tongue to feel the center of the hole, then BLOW. You can also put your fingertips on holes 2 and 3 on the left and 5 and 6 on the right. Remember the importance of hole 4, and practice BLOWING a clear note on it.

Note: Air must go directly into a single hole for a single note (see illustrations).

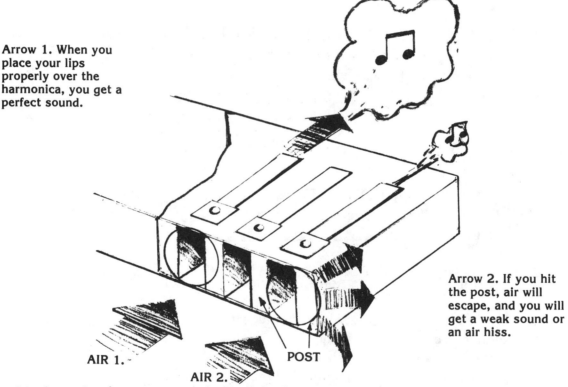

Arrow 1. When you place your lips properly over the harmonica, you get a perfect sound.

Arrow 2. If you hit the post, air will escape, and you will get a weak sound or an air hiss.

AIR 1.   POST
AIR 2.

11. Learning how to properly "lip" the harmonica gives you more control over all the effects you will be using later on. Lipping exercises pay off, especially when trying to attain advanced effects like bending notes.

To play Blues, Country, or Gospel.

Lipping

Pucker up and play just hole 4.

9

Try these next exercises at least the recommended number of times. And remember, the arrow up is BLOW and the arrow down is DRAW.

12. BLOW 1, 4, 10, 4, 1, 4, 10, five times.
↑ ↑ ↑ ↑ ↑ ↑ ↑

DRAW 1, 4, 10, 4, 1, 4, 10, five times and repeat another five.
↓ ↓ ↓ ↓ ↓ ↓ ↓

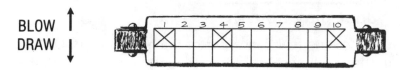

13. Be sure you are blowing and drawing individual notes.

BLOW 1, 2, 3, 4, and reverse to BLOW 4, 3, 2, 1, ten times.
↑ ↑ ↑ ↑   ↑ ↑ ↑ ↑

14. DRAW 1, 2, 3, 4, and reverse to DRAW 4, 3, 2, 1, ten times.
↓ ↓ ↓ ↓   ↓ ↓ ↓ ↓

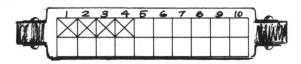

15. BLOW 1, 2, 3, 4, and reverse to DRAW 4, 3, 2, 1, ten times.
↑ ↑ ↑ ↑   ↓ ↓ ↓ ↓

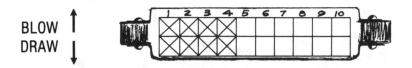

Remember to count the notes to yourself as you play.

16. Now see if you can BLOW hole 4 only, without using your fingers to block the neighboring holes, and without looking for the number. It might help to start at hole 1 and count up as you move to hole 4. Remember, you have to purse your lips to the size of a single hole to play single notes.

17. If you start on 4, first blowing then drawing the individual notes, and move up the scale repeating this on 5, 6, and 7, without DRAWING on 7 first, you will have played the C-major scale (assuming your harmonica is stamped with the key of C). Try this exercise thinking it should sound like do-re-mi-fa-sol-la-ti-do. Refer to the diagrams.

C-Major Scale

BLOW gently into hole 4, which is C (*do* on the diatonic musical scale).

Now DRAW from hole 4, which is D (*re*).

BLOW into hole 5, which is E (*mi*).

DRAW from hole 5, which is F (*fa*).

BLOW into hole 6, which is G (*sol*).

DRAW from hole 6, which is A (*la*).

DRAW from hole 7, which is B (*ti*).

BLOW into hole 7, which is C (*do*).

C harmonica in the diatonic scale.

C HARMONICA MIDDLE REGISTER

	HOLE NO.		NOTE
BLOW ↑	4	C	DO
DRAW ↓	4	D	RE
BLOW ↑	5	E	MI
DRAW ↓	5	F	FA
BLOW ↑	6	G	SOL
DRAW ↓	6	A	LA
DRAW ↓	7	B	TI
BLOW ↑	7	C	DO

Notice on hole 7 *the pattern changes*. You DRAW the first note, then you BLOW. You have now completed the diatonic 8-note scale (all the white notes on the piano.

18. When you move from one note to the next, notice how far apart they are. Get the feel of the spacing between them. BLOW holes 4, 7, 7, 4, seven times. DRAW holes 8, 8, 4, seven times. Are you getting the feel of it?

BLOW ↑
DRAW ↓

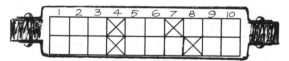

Remember, move the harmonica, not the lips.

19. Now let's play the scale from hole 7 to hole 4.

20. Now let's play the scale up and down. Practice this as many times as you can. Practice this until it becomes natural and easy for you. See how fast you can play.

BLOW ↑
DRAW ↓

C	D	E	F	G	A	B	C	B	A	G	F	E	D	C
↑	↓	↑	↓	↑	↓	↓	↑	↓	↓	↑	↓	↑	↓	↑
4	4	5	5	6	6	7	7	7	6	6	5	5	4	4

21. How long it will take you to gain this skill will depend on your effort and persistence. *Don't get discouraged.* This exercise will help your coordination with the instrument. There are thousands of songs written in this scale. Learn it well and you'll enjoy the harmonica for years to come.

22. Let us now concentrate on **breath,** which is your source of energy for playing the harmonica.

Take a deep breath and BLOW (exhale) into hole 1 as long as you can. Now without taking the harmonica from your lips, DRAW (inhale) as long as you can. Do this several times.

23. Move up to the next hole (hole 2) and repeat the exercise. Continue up to hole 10. Then repeat the exercise from hole 10 to hole 1. This will build up your playing ability. To increase your air, suck in, push, and use your diaphragm to get the maximum from each breath.

24. In the last exercise we discovered 4 more notes. They are hole 8 BLOW and DRAW, and hole 9 BLOW and DRAW.

Now you have played all 20 notes. Congratulations! You are well on your way!

BLOW ↑
DRAW ↓

25. When you go from one note to the next, don't pull the harmonica away from your lips to look at the notes. Always practice with two hands. If you have an old well worn harmonica, use it to experiment; then use your good one to play.

If you're playing more than one note at a time, you need to go back to the single-note steps for more practice. However, the harmonica is designed in such a way that if you sound two or more notes at a time, it won't seem discordant.

Make sure your lips are rounded and placed over the harmonica correctly.

Make sure you're listening to the notes.

Regardless of what hole number the song begins with, always start at blow hole 1 and count up to the start of the song, then blow or draw.

MARY HAD A LITTLE LAMB

All-time favorites you can play....
Straight-Harp Style

BLOW ↑
DRAW ↓

Because you know most of these songs, it will help you learn faster.

MICHAEL ROW YOUR BOAT ASHORE

C	E	G	E	G	A	G	E	G	A	G
↑	↑	↑	↑	↑	↓	↑	↑	↑	↓	↑
4	5	6	5	6	6	6	5	6	6	6

E	G	G	E	F	E	D	C	D	E	D	C
↑	↑	↑	↑	↓	↑	↓	↑	↓	↑	↓	↑
5	6	6	5	5	5	4	4	4	5	4	4

MARY HAD A LITTLE LAMB

E	D	C	D	E	E	E	D	D	D	E	G	G
↑	↓	↑	↓	↑	↑	↑	↓	↓	↓	↑	↑	↑
5	4	4	4	5	5	5	4	4	4	5	6	6

E	D	C	D	E	E	E	E	D	D	E	D	C
↑	↓	↑	↓	↑	↑	↑	↑	↓	↓	↑	↓	↑
5	4	4	4	5	5	5	5	4	4	5	4	4

FARMER IN THE DELL

G	C	C	C	C	C	D	E	E	E	E	E	F
↑	↑	↑	↑	↑	↑	↓	↑	↑	↑	↑	↑	↓
3	4	4	4	4	4	4	5	5	5	5	5	5

G	G	A	G	E	C	D	E	E	D	D	C
↑	↑	↓	↑	↑	↑	↓	↑	↑	↓	↓	↑
6	6	6	6	5	4	4	5	5	4	4	4

O SUSANA

Before starting songs, read page 28 about choking the reeds.

C	D	E	G	G	A	G	E	C	D	E	E	D	C	D
↑	↓	↑	↑	↑	↓	↑	↑	↑	↓	↑	↑	↓	↑	↓
4	4	5	6	6	6	6	5	4	4	5	5	4	4	4

C	D	E	G	G	A	G	E	C	D	E	E	D	D	C
↑	↓	↑	↑	↑	↓	↑	↑	↑	↓	↑	↑	↓	↓	↑
4	4	5	6	6	6	6	5	4	4	5	5	4	4	4

F	F	A	A	A	G	G	E	C	D
↓	↓	↓	↓	↓	↑	↑	↑	↑	↓
5	5	6	6	6	6	6	5	4	4

C	D	E	G	G	A	G	E	C	D	E	E	D	D	C
↑	↓	↑	↑	↑	↓	↑	↑	↑	↓	↑	↑	↓	↓	↑
4	4	5	6	6	6	6	5	4	4	5	5	4	4	4

All-time favorites you can play . . . . .

BLOW ↑
DRAW ↓

TWINKLE TWINKLE LITTLE STAR

C	C	G	G	A	A	G	F	F	E	E	D	D	C
↑	↑	↑	↑	↓	↑	↑	↓	↑	↑	↓	↑	↓	↑
4	4	6	6	6	6	6	5	5	5	5	4	4	4

G	G	F	F	E	E	D	G	G	F	F	E	E	D
↑	↑	↓	↑	↑	↓	↑	↑	↑	↓	↑	↑	↓	↓
6	6	5	5	5	5	4	6	6	5	5	5	5	4

C	C	G	G	A	A	G	F	F	E	E	D	D	C
↑	↑	↑	↑	↓	↓	↑	↓	↓	↓	↑	↑	↓	↑
4	4	6	6	6	6	6	5	5	5	5	4	4	4

GOOD NIGHT LADIES

E	C	G	C	E	C	D	D
↑	↑	↑	↑	↑	↑	↑	↓
5	4	3	4	5	4	4	4

E	C	F	F	F	E	E	D	D	C
↑	↑	↓	↓	↓	↑	↑	↓	↓	↑
5	4	5	5	5	5	5	4	4	4

FRERE JACQUES

C	D	E	C	C	D	E	C	E	F	G	E	F	G	G	A	G
↑	↓	↑	↑	↑	↓	↑	↑	↑	↓	↑	↑	↓	↑	↑	↓	↑
4	4	5	4	4	4	5	4	5	5	6	5	5	6	6	6	6

F	E	C	G	A	G	F	E	C	C	G	C	C	G	C
↓	↑	↑	↑	↓	↑	↓	↑	↑	↑	↑	↑	↑	↑	↑
5	5	4	6	6	6	5	5	4	4	3	4	4	3	4

THREE BLIND MICE

E	D	C	E	D	C	G	F	F	E	G	F	F	E	G	C	C	B	A	B	C	G	G
↑	↓	↑	↑	↓	↑	↑	↓	↓	↑	↑	↓	↓	↑	↑	↑	↑	↓	↓	↓	↑	↑	↑
5	4	4	5	4	4	6	5	5	5	6	5	5	5	6	7	7	7	6	7	7	6	6

G	C	C	B	A	B	C	G	G	G	C	C	B	A	B	C	G	G	F	E	D	C
↑	↑	↑	↓	↓	↓	↑	↑	↑	↑	↑	↑	↓	↓	↓	↑	↑	↑	↓	↑	↓	↑
6	7	7	7	6	7	7	6	6	6	7	7	7	6	7	7	6	6	5	5	4	4

All-time favorites you can play . . . .

BLOW ↑
DRAW ↓

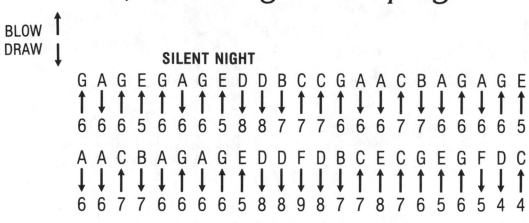

SILENT NIGHT

G A G E G A G E D D B C C G A A C B A G A G E
↑ ↓ ↑ ↑ ↑ ↓ ↑ ↑ ↓ ↓ ↑ ↑ ↑ ↑ ↓ ↓ ↑ ↑ ↓ ↑ ↓ ↑ ↑
6 6 6 5 6 6 6 5 8 8 7 7 7 6 6 6 7 7 6 6 6 6 5

A A C B A G A G E D D F D B C E C G E G F D C
↓ ↓ ↑ ↑ ↓ ↑ ↓ ↑ ↑ ↓ ↓ ↓ ↓ ↑ ↑ ↑ ↑ ↑ ↑ ↑ ↓ ↓ ↑
6 6 7 7 6 6 6 6 5 8 8 9 8 7 7 8 7 6 5 6 6 4 4

ALOUETTE

C D E E D C D E C G C D E E D C D E C
↑ ↓ ↑ ↑ ↓ ↑ ↓ ↑ ↑ ↑ ↑ ↓ ↑ ↑ ↓ ↑ ↓ ↑ ↑
4 4 5 5 4 4 4 5 4 3 4 4 5 5 4 4 4 5 4

C C C E G G G G G E G G G G G G
↑ ↑ ↑ ↑ ↑ ↑ ↑ ↑ ↑ ↑ ↑ ↑ ↑ ↑ ↑ ↑
4 4 4 5 6 6 6 6 6 5 3 3 3 6 6 6

WHEN THE SAINTS GO MARCHING IN

C E F G C E F G C E F G E C E D
↑ ↑ ↓ ↑ ↑ ↑ ↓ ↑ ↑ ↑ ↓ ↑ ↑ ↑ ↑ ↓
4 5 5 6 4 5 5 6 4 5 5 6 5 4 5 4

E E D C C E G G F E F G E C D C
↑ ↑ ↓ ↑ ↑ ↑ ↑ ↑ ↓ ↑ ↓ ↑ ↑ ↑ ↓ ↑
5 5 4 4 4 5 6 6 5 5 5 6 5 4 4 4

LONDON BRIDGE

G A G F E F G D E F E F
↑ ↓ ↑ ↓ ↑ ↓ ↑ ↓ ↑ ↓ ↓ ↓
6 6 6 5 5 5 6 4 5 5 5 5

G G A G F E F G D G E C
↑ ↑ ↓ ↑ ↓ ↑ ↓ ↑ ↓ ↑ ↑ ↑
6 6 6 6 5 5 5 6 4 6 5 4

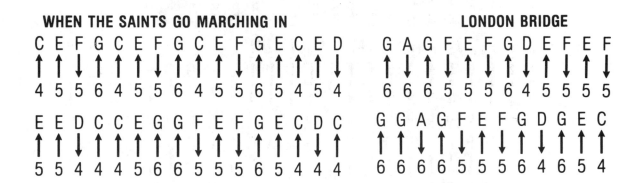

ON TOP OF OLD SMOKEY

C C E G C A F F G A G C C E G G D E F E D C
↑ ↑ ↑ ↑ ↑ ↓ ↓ ↓ ↑ ↓ ↑ ↑ ↑ ↑ ↑ ↑ ↓ ↑ ↓ ↑ ↓ ↑
4 4 5 6 7 6 5 5 6 6 6 4 4 5 6 6 4 5 5 5 4 4

All-time favorites you can play . . . .

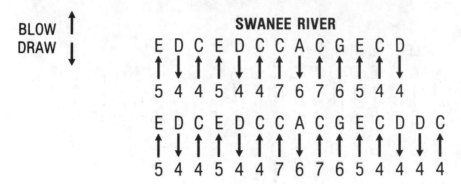

BLOW ↑
DRAW ↓

SWANEE RIVER

```
E D C E D C C A C G E C D
↑ ↓ ↑ ↑ ↓ ↑ ↑ ↓ ↑ ↓ ↑ ↑ ↓
5 4 4 5 4 4 7 6 7 6 5 4 4

E D C E D C C A C G E C D D C
↑ ↓ ↑ ↑ ↓ ↑ ↑ ↓ ↑ ↓ ↑ ↑ ↓ ↓ ↑
5 4 4 5 4 4 7 6 7 6 5 4 4 4 4
```

OLD MACDONALD HAD A FARM

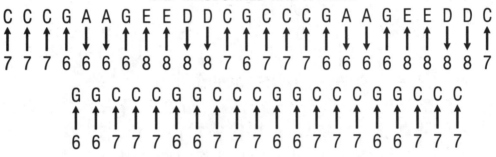

```
C C C G A A G E E D D C G C C C G A A G E E D D C
↑ ↑ ↑ ↑ ↓ ↓ ↑ ↓ ↓ ↓ ↓ ↑ ↓ ↑ ↑ ↑ ↑ ↓ ↓ ↑ ↓ ↓ ↓ ↓ ↑
7 7 7 6 6 6 6 8 8 8 8 7 6 7 7 7 6 6 6 6 8 8 8 8 7
```

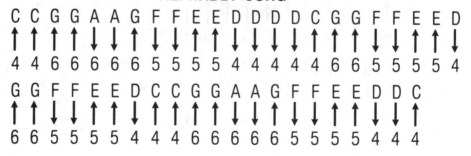

```
G G C C C G G C C C G G C C C G G C C C
↑ ↑ ↑ ↑ ↑ ↑ ↑ ↑ ↑ ↑ ↑ ↑ ↑ ↑ ↑ ↑ ↑ ↑ ↑ ↑
6 6 7 7 7 6 6 7 7 7 6 6 7 7 7 6 6 7 7 7
```

```
C C C G A A G E E D D C
↑ ↑ ↑ ↑ ↓ ↓ ↑ ↓ ↓ ↓ ↓ ↑
7 7 7 6 6 6 6 8 8 8 8 7
```

ALPHABET SONG

```
C C G G A A G F F E E D D D D C G G F F E E D
↑ ↑ ↑ ↑ ↓ ↓ ↑ ↓ ↓ ↑ ↑ ↓ ↓ ↓ ↓ ↑ ↑ ↑ ↓ ↓ ↑ ↑ ↓
4 4 6 6 6 6 6 5 5 5 5 4 4 4 4 4 6 6 5 5 5 5 4

G G F F E E D C C G G A A G F F E E D D C
↑ ↑ ↓ ↓ ↑ ↑ ↓ ↑ ↑ ↑ ↑ ↓ ↓ ↑ ↓ ↓ ↑ ↑ ↓ ↓ ↑
6 6 5 5 5 5 4 4 4 6 6 6 6 6 5 5 5 5 4 4 4
```

JOY TO THE WORLD

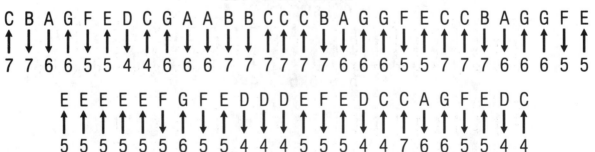

```
C B A G F E D C G A A B B C C C B A G G G F E C C B A G G F E
↑ ↓ ↑ ↑ ↓ ↑ ↓ ↑ ↓ ↑ ↑ ↓ ↓ ↑ ↑ ↑ ↓ ↑ ↑ ↑ ↓ ↑ ↑ ↑ ↓ ↑ ↑ ↑ ↓ ↓ ↑
7 7 6 6 5 5 4 4 6 6 6 7 7 7 7 7 6 6 6 5 5 7 7 7 6 6 6 6 5 5 5

E E E E E F G F E D D D E F E D C C A G F E D C
↑ ↑ ↑ ↑ ↑ ↓ ↑ ↓ ↑ ↓ ↓ ↓ ↑ ↓ ↑ ↓ ↑ ↑ ↓ ↑ ↓ ↑ ↓ ↑
5 5 5 5 5 5 5 5 5 4 4 4 5 5 4 4 7 6 6 5 5 4 4
```

16

All-time favorites you can play....

BLOW ↑
DRAW ↓

DIXIE

G	E	C	C	C	D	E	F	G	G	G	E	A	G	A	G	A	B	C	D	E
↑	↑	↑	↑	↑	↓	↑	↓	↑	↑	↑	↓	↑	↓	↑	↓	↑	↑	↓	↓	↑
6	5	4	4	4	5	5	6	6	6	5	6	6	6	6	6	6	7	7	8	8

C	G	C	G	E	G	D	E	C	G	C	E	D	C	A	C	A	D	A	D
↑	↑	↑	↑	↑	↑	↓	↑	↑	↑	↑	↑	↓	↑	↓	↑	↓	↓	↓	↓
7	6	7	6	5	6	4	5	4	6	7	8	8	7	6	7	6	8	6	8

G	C	E	D	C	A	B	C	A	G	E	C	E	E	D	E	D	C	E	D	A	G	E	E	D	D	C
↑	↑	↑	↓	↑	↓	↑	↓	↑	↑	↑	↑	↓	↑	↓	↑	↓	↑	↓	↓	↑	↑	↓	↓	↓	↓	↑
6	7	8	8	7	6	7	8	6	6	5	7	5	5	4	5	4	4	5	4	6	6	5	8	8	8	7

YANKEE DOODLE

C	C	D	E	C	E	D	G	C	C	D	E	C	B	G	C	C	D	E	F	E	D	C	B	G	A	B	C	C
↑	↑	↓	↑	↑	↓	↓	↑	↑	↑	↓	↑	↑	↓	↑	↑	↑	↓	↑	↑	↓	↓	↑	↓	↑	↓	↓	↑	↑
7	7	8	8	7	8	8	6	7	7	8	8	7	7	6	7	7	8	8	9	8	8	7	7	6	6	7	7	7

A	B	A	G	A	B	C	G	A	G	F	E	G	A	B	A	G	A	B	C	A	G	C	D	E	C	C
↓	↓	↓	↑	↓	↓	↑	↑	↓	↑	↓	↑	↑	↓	↓	↓	↑	↓	↓	↑	↓	↑	↑	↓	↑	↓	↑
6	7	6	6	6	7	7	6	6	6	5	5	6	6	7	6	6	6	7	7	6	6	7	8	7	7	7

THIS OLD MAN

G	E	G	G	E	G	A	G	F	E	D	E	F
↑	↑	↑	↑	↑	↑	↓	↓	↓	↓	↓	↓	↓
6	5	6	6	5	6	6	6	5	5	4	5	5

E	F	G	C	C	C	C	C	D	E	F	G	G	D	D	F	E	D	C
↑	↓	↑	↑	↑	↑	↑	↑	↓	↑	↓	↑	↑	↓	↓	↓	↑	↓	↑
5	5	6	4	4	4	4	4	5	5	6	6	4	4	5	5	4	4

AMAZING GRACE

G	C	E	D	C	E	D	C	D	C	A	G	G	A	C	E	D	C	E	D	E	G	E	G	G
↑	↑	↑	↓	↑	↑	↓	↑	↓	↑	↑	↑	↑	↑	↑	↑	↓	↑	↑	↓	↑	↑	↑	↑	↑
6	7	8	8	7	8	8	7	8	7	6	6	6	6	7	8	8	7	8	8	8	9	8	9	9

E	G	A	E	F	E	D	C	D	C	A	G	G	A	C	E	D	C	E	D	C
↑	↑	↑	↓	↓	↑	↓	↑	↓	↑	↑	↑	↑	↑	↑	↑	↓	↑	↑	↓	↑
8	9	10	8	9	8	8	7	8	7	6	6	6	6	7	8	8	7	8	8	7

All-time favorites you can play....

BLOW ↑
DRAW ↓

HOME ON THE RANGE

```
G  G  C  D  E  C  B  A  F  F  F  E  F  G  C  C  C  B  C  D
↑  ↑  ↑  ↓  ↑  ↑  ↑  ↓  ↓  ↓  ↓  ↑  ↓  ↑  ↑  ↑  ↓  ↑  ↓  ↓
6  6  7  8  8  7  7  6  9  9  9  8  9  9  7  7  7  7  7  8

G  G  C  D  E  C  B  A  F  F  F  F  F  E  D  C  B  C  D  C
↑  ↑  ↑  ↓  ↑  ↑  ↑  ↓  ↓  ↓  ↓  ↓  ↓  ↑  ↓  ↑  ↑  ↓  ↓  ↑
6  6  7  8  8  7  7  6  9  9  9  9  9  8  8  7  7  7  8  7

G  F  E  D  E  G  C  C  C  B  C  D  G  G  C  D  E
↑  ↓  ↑  ↓  ↑  ↑  ↑  ↑  ↑  ↓  ↑  ↓  ↑  ↑  ↑  ↓  ↑
9  9  8  8  8  6  7  7  7  7  7  8  6  6  6  7  8  8

C  B  A  F  F  F  F  F  E  D  C  B  C  D  C
↑  ↓  ↓  ↓  ↓  ↓  ↓  ↓  ↑  ↓  ↑  ↓  ↑  ↓  ↑
7  7  6  9  9  9  9  9  8  8  7  7  7  8  7
```

BLOW THE MAN DOWN

```
G  G  A  G  E  C  E  G  A  G  E  C  E  G  A  F  E  F  D
↑  ↑  ↓  ↑  ↑  ↑  ↑  ↑  ↓  ↑  ↑  ↑  ↑  ↑  ↓  ↓  ↑  ↓  ↓
6  6  6  6  5  4  5  6  6  6  5  4  5  6  6  5  5  5  4

F  G  F  D  B  D  F  G  F  D  B  D  F  G  E  D  E  C
↓  ↑  ↓  ↓  ↓  ↓  ↓  ↑  ↓  ↓  ↓  ↓  ↓  ↑  ↑  ↓  ↑  ↑
5  6  5  4  3  4  5  6  5  4  3  4  5  6  5  4  5  4
```

DECK THE HALLS

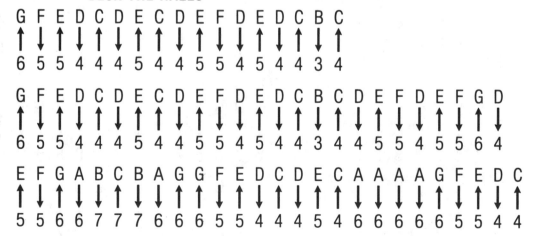

```
G  F  E  D  C  D  E  C  D  E  F  D  E  D  C  B  C
↑  ↓  ↑  ↓  ↑  ↓  ↑  ↑  ↓  ↑  ↓  ↓  ↑  ↓  ↑  ↓  ↑
6  5  5  4  4  4  5  4  4  5  5  4  5  4  4  3  4

G  F  E  D  C  D  E  C  D  E  F  D  E  D  C  B  C  D  E  F  D  E  F  G  D
↑  ↓  ↑  ↓  ↑  ↓  ↑  ↑  ↓  ↑  ↓  ↓  ↑  ↓  ↑  ↓  ↑  ↓  ↑  ↓  ↓  ↑  ↓  ↑  ↓
6  5  5  4  4  4  5  4  4  5  5  4  5  4  4  3  4  4  5  5  4  5  5  6  4

E  F  G  A  B  C  B  A  G  G  F  E  D  C  D  E  C  A  A  A  G  F  E  D  C
↑  ↓  ↑  ↓  ↓  ↑  ↓  ↓  ↑  ↑  ↓  ↑  ↓  ↑  ↓  ↑  ↑  ↓  ↓  ↓  ↑  ↓  ↑  ↓  ↑
5  5  6  6  7  7  7  6  6  6  5  5  4  4  4  5  4  6  6  6  6  5  5  4  4
```

All-time favorites you can play . . . .

BLOW ↑
DRAW ↓

YELLOW ROSE OF TEXAS

G F E G G G A G G F E G C D E G G G E E F E D C C D E D
↑ ↓ ↑ ↑ ↑ ↓ ↑ ↑ ↑ ↓ ↑ ↑ ↑ ↓ ↑ ↑ ↑ ↑ ↑ ↑ ↓ ↑ ↓ ↑ ↑ ↓ ↑ ↓
6 5 5 6 6 6 6 6 6 5 5 6 7 8 8 6 6 6 8 9 8 8 7 7 8 8 8

G F E G G G A G G F E G C D E G G A F F E E D C G G E E D C
↑ ↓ ↑ ↑ ↑ ↓ ↑ ↑ ↑ ↓ ↑ ↑ ↑ ↓ ↑ ↑ ↑ ↓ ↓ ↓ ↑ ↑ ↓ ↑ ↑ ↑ ↑ ↑ ↓ ↑
6 5 5 6 6 6 6 6 6 5 5 6 7 8 8 6 6 6 9 9 8 8 8 7 6 6 8 8 8 7

WE WISH YOU A MERRY CHRISTMAS

G C C D C B A A A D D E D C B G G E E F E D C A G G A D B C
↑ ↑ ↑ ↑ ↑ ↓ ↓ ↓ ↓ ↑ ↑ ↓ ↑ ↑ ↓ ↑ ↑ ↑ ↑ ↓ ↑ ↑ ↓ ↑ ↑ ↑ ↑ ↓ ↓ ↑
6 7 7 8 7 7 6 6 6 8 8 8 8 7 7 6 6 8 8 9 8 8 7 6 6 6 6 8 7 7

SHE'LL BE COMING AROUND THE MOUNTAIN

G A C C C C A G G A C C D E E E E G E D C D G F
↑ ↓ ↑ ↑ ↑ ↑ ↓ ↑ ↑ ↓ ↑ ↑ ↓ ↑ ↑ ↑ ↑ ↑ ↑ ↓ ↑ ↓ ↑ ↓
6 6 7 7 7 7 6 6 6 6 7 7 8 8 8 8 8 9 8 8 7 8 9 9

E E E E D C C B A A A A D C B A G G G G E D A B C
↑ ↑ ↑ ↑ ↓ ↑ ↑ ↓ ↓ ↓ ↓ ↓ ↑ ↑ ↓ ↓ ↑ ↑ ↑ ↑ ↑ ↓ ↓ ↓ ↑
8 8 8 8 8 7 7 7 6 6 6 6 8 7 7 6 6 6 6 6 8 8 6 7 7

TOM DOOLEY

G G G A C E E
↑ ↑ ↑ ↓ ↑ ↑ ↑
6 6 6 6 7 8 8

G G G A C D
↑ ↑ ↑ ↓ ↑ ↓
6 6 6 6 7 8

G G G A C D D
↑ ↑ ↑ ↓ ↑ ↓ ↓
6 6 6 7 8 8 8

D D E C A C
↓ ↓ ↑ ↑ ↓ ↑
8 8 8 7 6 7

MY DARLING CLEMENTINE

C C C G E E E C C E G G F E D
↑ ↑ ↑ ↑ ↑ ↑ ↑ ↑ ↑ ↑ ↑ ↑ ↓ ↑ ↓
7 7 7 6 8 8 8 7 7 8 9 9 9 8 8

D E F F F E D E C G C E D G B D C
↓ ↑ ↓ ↓ ↓ ↑ ↓ ↑ ↑ ↑ ↑ ↑ ↓ ↑ ↓ ↓ ↑
8 8 9 9 9 8 8 8 7 6 7 8 8 6 7 8 7

19

All-time favorites you can play . . . .

BLOW ↑
DRAW ↓

FOR HE'S A JOLLY GOOD FELLOW

C	E	E	E	D	E	F	E	E	D	D	C	D	E	C	D	E	E	E	D	E	F	A	A	G	G	G	F	D	C
↑	↑	↑	↑	↓	↑	↑	↑	↑	↓	↓	↑	↓	↑	↑	↓	↑	↑	↑	↓	↑	↑	↓	↓	↑	↑	↑	↓	↓	↑
7	8	8	8	8	8	9	8	8	8	8	7	8	8	7	8	8	8	8	8	8	9	10	10	9	9	9	9	8	7

E	G	G	G	A	A	G	G	E	E	F	F	E	C	D	E	E	E	D	E	F	A	A	G	G	G	F	D	C
↑	↑	↑	↑	↓	↓	↑	↑	↑	↑	↑	↑	↑	↑	↓	↑	↑	↑	↓	↑	↑	↓	↓	↑	↑	↑	↓	↓	↑
8	9	9	9	10	10	9	9	8	8	8	8	9	9	8	7	8	8	8	8	8	9	10	10	9	9	9	9	8	7

WILDWOOD FLOWER

E	F	G	A	C	E	F	E	D	E	D	C	E	F	G	A	C	E	F	E	D	E	D	C
↑	↓	↑	↑	↑	↑	↓	↑	↓	↑	↓	↑	↑	↓	↑	↑	↑	↑	↓	↑	↓	↑	↓	↑
5	5	6	6	7	5	5	5	4	5	4	4	5	5	6	6	7	5	5	5	4	5	4	4

G	A	E	E	D	C	G	A	G	A	G	E	F	G	A	C	E	F	E	D	E	D	C
↑	↓	↑	↑	↓	↑	↑	↓	↑	↓	↑	↑	↓	↑	↑	↑	↑	↓	↑	↓	↑	↓	↑
6	6	8	8	8	7	6	6	7	6	6	5	5	6	6	7	5	5	5	4	5	4	4

I'VE BEEN WORKING ON THE RAILROAD

C	G	C	G	C	D	E	C	F	F	C	D	E	C	G	C	G	C	D	E	C	E	E	E	D	D	E	D
↑	↑	↑	↑	↑	↓	↑	↑	↓	↓	↑	↓	↑	↑	↑	↑	↑	↑	↓	↑	↑	↑	↑	↑	↓	↓	↑	↓
7	6	7	6	7	8	8	7	9	9	7	8	8	7	6	7	6	7	8	8	7	8	8	8	8	8	8	8

D	C	D	C	E	D	C	G	F	F	C	D	E	A	B	C	B	C	A	G	C	E	F	E	D	C
↓	↑	↓	↑	↑	↓	↑	↑	↓	↓	↑	↓	↑	↓	↓	↑	↓	↑	↓	↑	↑	↑	↓	↑	↓	↑
8	7	8	7	8	8	7	6	9	9	7	8	8	6	7	7	7	7	6	6	7	8	9	8	8	7

G	G	G	G	C	A	A	A	D	C	B	B	B	B	A	B	C	D	E	G	G	G	C
↑	↑	↑	↑	↑	↓	↓	↓	↓	↑	↓	↓	↓	↓	↓	↓	↑	↓	↑	↑	↑	↑	↑
6	6	6	6	7	6	6	6	8	7	7	7	7	7	6	7	7	8	8	6	6	6	7

A	A	A	A	D	C	B	B	B	B	A	B	C
↓	↓	↓	↓	↓	↑	↓	↓	↓	↓	↓	↓	↑
6	6	6	6	8	7	7	7	7	7	6	7	7

20

All-time favorites you can play. . . .

BLOW ↑
DRAW ↓

JINGLE BELLS

G E D C G G G G E D C A A F E D B G G F D E
↑ ↑ ↓ ↓ ↑ ↑ ↑ ↑ ↑ ↓ ↓ ↓ ↓ ↓ ↑ ↓ ↓ ↑ ↑ ↓ ↓ ↑
6 8 8 7 6 6 6 6 8 8 7 6 6 9 8 8 7 9 9 9 8 8

G E D C G G E D C A A A F E D G G G G A G F D C
↑ ↑ ↓ ↓ ↑ ↑ ↑ ↓ ↓ ↓ ↓ ↓ ↓ ↑ ↓ ↑ ↑ ↑ ↑ ↑ ↑ ↓ ↓ ↑
6 8 8 7 6 6 6 8 8 7 6 6 6 8 8 9 9 9 9 10 9 9 8 7

G E E E E E E G C D E F F F F E E E E D D E D G
↑ ↑ ↑ ↑ ↑ ↑ ↑ ↑ ↑ ↓ ↓ ↓ ↓ ↓ ↓ ↑ ↑ ↑ ↑ ↓ ↓ ↑ ↓ ↑
9 8 8 8 8 8 8 9 7 8 8 9 9 9 9 9 8 8 8 8 8 8 8 9

E E E E E G C D E F F F F F E E E G G F D C
↑ ↑ ↑ ↑ ↑ ↑ ↑ ↑ ↑ ↓ ↓ ↓ ↓ ↓ ↓ ↑ ↑ ↑ ↑ ↑ ↓ ↓ ↑
8 8 8 8 8 8 9 7 8 8 9 9 9 9 9 8 8 8 9 9 9 8 7

RED RIVER VALLEY

G C E E E D E D C G C E C E G F E D
↑ ↑ ↑ ↑ ↑ ↑ ↓ ↓ ↑ ↓ ↑ ↑ ↑ ↑ ↑ ↑ ↓ ↑ ↓
6 7 8 8 8 8 8 8 7 6 7 8 7 8 9 9 8 8

G F E E D C D E G F A A G B C D E D C
↑ ↓ ↑ ↑ ↓ ↓ ↓ ↑ ↑ ↓ ↓ ↓ ↑ ↓ ↑ ↑ ↓ ↓ ↑
9 9 8 8 8 7 8 8 9 9 6 6 6 7 7 8 8 8 7

O COME ALL YE FAITHFUL

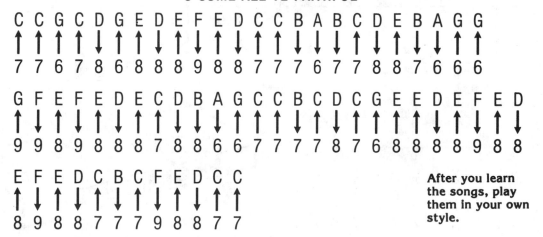

C C G C D G E D E F E D C C B A B C D E B A G G
↑ ↑ ↑ ↑ ↑ ↑ ↓ ↑ ↓ ↓ ↓ ↑ ↓ ↑ ↓ ↓ ↑ ↑ ↓ ↑ ↓ ↓ ↑ ↑
7 7 6 7 8 6 8 8 9 8 8 7 7 7 6 7 7 8 8 7 6 6

G F E F E D E C D B A G C C B C D C G E E D E F E D
↑ ↓ ↑ ↓ ↑ ↓ ↑ ↑ ↓ ↓ ↓ ↑ ↑ ↑ ↓ ↑ ↓ ↑ ↑ ↑ ↑ ↓ ↑ ↓ ↑ ↓
9 9 8 9 8 8 8 7 8 8 6 6 7 7 7 7 8 7 6 8 8 8 8 9 8 8

E F E D C B C F E D C C
↑ ↓ ↑ ↓ ↑ ↓ ↑ ↓ ↑ ↓ ↑ ↑
8 9 8 8 7 7 7 9 8 8 7 7

After you learn
the songs, play
them in your own
style.

21

SECTION II

GETTING GOOD

IF you have completed and practiced the first section, or if you are ALREADY advanced enough to play the individual notes of a major scale, then you are ready for this section. You can browse and take it a bit at a time, if you like, because this section is made of simple "modules" designed to teach tricks and techniques of the pros. Most of the modules or subsections are self-contained to make it easy for you to gain the certain effect you want. Whether you want to work on scales, chords, harmonizing effects, or "bending" notes is up to you. But for best results, follow the sequence as it is presented, skipping only what you have already mastered.

Straight Harp

"Straight harp" is the three diatonic "C" scales we have just learned on our C harmonica and are known as the "blow position" or "straight harp" style.

Straight harp means that the piano and guitar will play in the key of C and you will play in C also. You can use all three C scales—lower, middle and upper register. Look at the letter "C" on the harp plate. When you say "straight harp," you are referring to the key the harmonica is in.

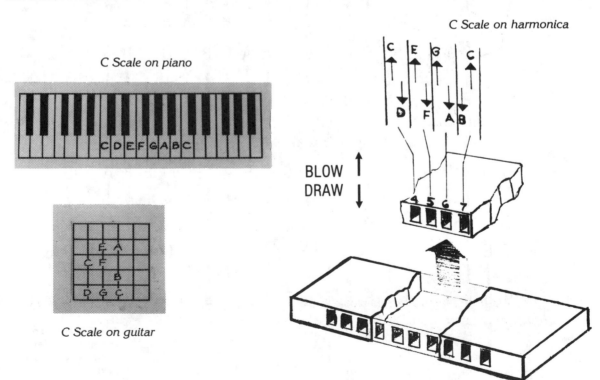

C Scale on piano

C Scale on guitar

C Scale on harmonica

BLOW ↑
DRAW ↓

Register Location

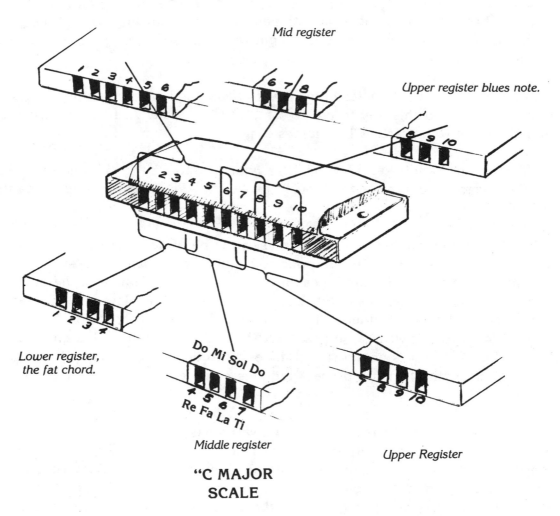

To play blues notes,
bend notes on holes 1 to 6 by drawing.

Mid register

Upper register blues note.

Lower register,
the fat chord.

Do Mi Sol Do

Re Fa La Ti

Middle register

Upper Register

"C MAJOR
SCALE

The 10-hole Harmonica is designed so that when you BLOW, you play a full C MAJOR chord, and when you DRAW, you play G⁷, the DOMINATE CHORD.

Cross Harp and Note Bending

Cross harp, *second* position and *draw* position all refer to the same playing technique. You play the same C harmonica, but instead of using the C scale as your "base," you will play in the key of G, the *blues* scale or mixolidian mode.

As almost anyone who has ever had a brief romance with the harmonica knows, there are some notes on the diatonic scale that are apparently not available on the standard three-octave instrument. Those "missing" notes *are* recoverable, however, to the player who wants to become serious about creating real music with the harmonica.

The concept for deliberate note alteration is called "bending" or "choking"; it is a technique for drawing or blowing in a controlled way to lower or raise the register of specific   notes.

There are two missing notes in the lower register and one in the upper register that must be produced this way to create a full musical scale. At first, the process feels unnatural; but with practice, it becomes easy.

Notes can be bent in several ways. It's a good idea to experiment, and then settle on the method that seems easiest for you. I'll explain how I do it, so you may have a starting point.

First, it is important to know which notes can be bent and which ones *can't* be. No, all notes on the harmonica do *not* respond to bending in the same way—which probably explains why most casual harmonica players never become familiar with note bending. In the lower register, for holes 1 through 6, note bending is achieved by drawing. Hole 3 is the most "flexible" of them all, and permits a tonal spread of no less than three chromatic steps! It is virtually impossible to bend the note at hole 7. Depending on the key you're using, notes obtained from holes 5 through 10 are bent by blowing. In the upper register, the bending process requires considerably greater air pressure than normal.

An easy way to get the feel of the sound variations available from a single note is to tilt the back part of your harp up and down as you draw on a single note in the lower register. Don't try to change your mouthing technique at this point; merely create a note by drawing in air and continue to alternate the tilt position of the instrument—up and down. Note that this tilting changes the direction of the source of air passing over the reed, which changes the air pressure and causes it to vibrate at a two distinctly different pitches.

Once you've achieved the tonal variation on a single note, you're ready to start practicing other techniques that allow you to create this note shift more naturally.

24

Some Extra Help in Bending Notes

If you're having trouble getting those bends right, some of these tips might help. Let's take it from the low end of the scale, and work on DRAW hole 2. Tighten the lips to direct the air into *hole 2 only.* Using twice the air needed to play a regular note, draw and tilt slowly. Try to get coordination between your hand motion and breath control. You should be able to hear a slight difference. Notice that the sound is higher when the instrument is tilted upward and lower when moved down. Practice this a few times until you can hear the sound changes of the bent note.

To produce the bent notes with your mouth, a combination of things must happen which will alter the mouth chamber. You will discover what is right for you by experimenting, because no two mouths are alike. The objective is to change the air flow in such a way as to change the reed vibration rate.

Using the lipping technique on hole 2 only, tighten all of the muscles in your mouth and jaw so that the air is being forced through a much narrower passage than is normally used. Try to become aware of what is happening: The lower jaw comes forward, lowering the tone. The tongue touches the roof of the mouth. The cheeks and throat actually pull the note through the inner cavity as the tongue tightens and moves back. The middle part of the tongue touches the upper part of the mouth.

In your deepest voice practice saying "EE-O, EE-O"* a few times. Notice how the muscles move inside your mouth and how the air chamber changes shape and size. Now duplicate these motions by preparing your mouth as if to say "EE-O, EE-O" as you DRAW on hole 2. Experiment! Find the shape that gives the desired sounds or bends. The deeper the "EE" the more effect it will have. The tightened lips, tongue dropping and rising, coupled with increased air velocity controlled by the diaphragm is what puts more pressure on the reed and changes the sound. Even greater pressure can be obtained by placing the index finger on the back of the harmonica.

A word of caution is needed here. In order to bend properly, greater air pressure is needed. Care must be taken not to overblow or draw incorrectly, because too much force can damage the reeds, causing them to get out of tune (or bend out of shape) permanently. Practice is the best way to learn how much is enough. Try to practice on an old harmonica first.

As you practice bending notes, you may notice your mouth getting tired or that you run out of breath. This is because your muscles are not used to forming these shapes and straining in this way. *Don't overdo it.* Rest awhile, then try again. Practice will build up strength in your jaws and mouth so that soon it will be easy and comfortable to bend any note you desire.

*If EE-O doesn't work, try TE-O.

Practice can be compared to any exercise for strengthening muscles, such as weight lifting or marathon running: It will do the job of building the exercised muscles, but not without the fatigue that comes first; it's the price we pay.

Practice DRAWING on hole 2, dropping and raising the tongue until it is easy to produce a clear sound, alternating the pitch gradually up and down. This is the way you master CONTROL of the bendable notes. Notice that the original note is restored when the mouth is relaxed and returns to the normal drawing position.

On *bend* hole 2 we have three chromatic half steps—three distinctly different notes—we can play. Hold hole 2 DRAW. You get G, F$^{\#}$ and F by varying your bending. F is one of the most important missing notes on the harp, and learning to play it is essential if you're serious about mastering this instrument. Hole 2 DRAW is used to play the F in the lower register *straight* harp and is used to play the *blues* note in the key of G *cross* harp.

Hole 2

DRAW
HALF BEND
FULL BEND

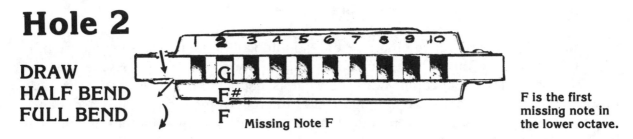

F is the first missing note in the lower octave.

On hole 3 DRAW, you can get *three* chromatic half steps! DRAW at hole 3 for B, then *bend slightly* to lower the pitch to B♭; then give a *full* bend to get "A".

Hole 3

DRAW
HALF BEND
FULL BEND

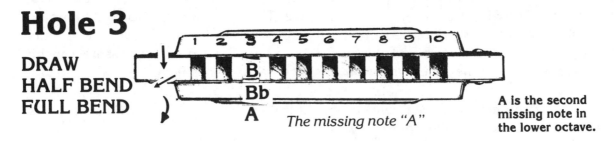

The missing note "A"

A is the second missing note in the lower octave.

"A" was the second missing note in the lower diatonic octave. DRAW hole 4 is D. Bend it to get D♭. On holes 1 and 4 you can get D and D♭. D♭ is the missing note on both hole 1 and hole 4.

Hole 1

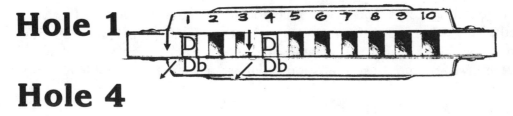

Hole 4

It is possible to bend two notes simultaneously at draw hole 2 and draw hole 3. Before drawing hole 2 for G you must draw it extra hard to lower the pitch enough to make the full transition from G to F. Practice bending from F to G and A to B back and forth *repeatedly* until you have it mastered.

Lower Register

To hear what F should sound like, draw hole 5 and hole 9. They are the same note, even though they are an octave apart on the scale.

To complete the diatonic scale on the lower register in holes 1, 2, 3 and 4, there are two missing notes. They are on DRAW hole 2 and DRAW hole 3—F and A in the key of C, and are full bends. Play BLOW hole 1 which is C, DRAW hole 1 which is D, BLOW hole 2 which is E, DRAW hole 2 which is G. We need to get the note in between, which is F. [We have to learn to DRAW bend hole 2 to get the F. To find F, it's in draw hole 5 and hole 9 shown in the illustration.] To get F, the missing note, we have to draw on hole 2 and *really suck it in!*   **Look at Diagram 42A**

(The missing note "A" to complete the lower register can be found in hole 6 DRAW. In the upper register, it is hole 10). When you are choking the note you are changing the airflow and causing the reed to vibrate in a different way, producing a different sound.

"F" and "A" are the two missing notes in the Lower Register.

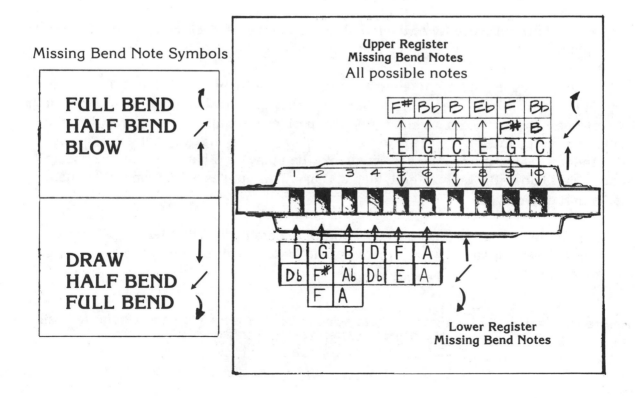

27

Choking Harmonica Reeds

Muffled or whining sounds, lowering of a tone, and no sound at all are problems encountered by most harmonica players occasionally. This is referred to as "choking your reeds." Generally, these problems are caused by one of the following:

1. Forcing too much air through the reed and sound chamber.

2. Incorrect position of the tongue when using the lip playing method.

3. Incorrect shape of the interior of your mouth when using the tongue blocking method.

These incorrect practices do not allow the reeds to function properly. The following will help you to avoid choking reeds:

1. For a reed to vibrate freely, the airflow through the reed and its sound chamber must be smooth and not forced or pushed.

2. Your tongue should be down and placed lightly against the bottom of the gums. Lifting the tongue will result in a lowering of the tone.

3. The hollow of the cavity of the mouth should be lengthened by dropping the jaw slightly.

Since each reed is a different length, one must adjust the volume of his attack when playing different notes. There are certain notes that continually create frustration for harp players. The low notes which create more problems require more volume than the higher notes. You must learn to make adjustments when playing different notes on your instrument. One must have the correct attack when playing a harmonica. It may seem impossible to do until you master it, then it's easy. This applies to any wind instrument that is properly played.

The harmonica must be approached with the understanding that technique plays a major role. Only patience and practice can resolve difficulties in playing this instrument.   *Courtesy Hohner Harmonica Co.*

Before attempting to play the cross-harp selections, please turn to page 12 and read all the material included under step 25.

All-time favorites you can play . . . .
Cross-Harp Style

Listen to the cassette tape while you are playing these songs.

MICHAEL ROW YOUR BOAT ASHORE

G B D B D E D B D E D
↓ ↓ ↓ ↓ ↓ ↑ ↓ ↓ ↓ ↑ ↓
2 3 4 3 3 5 4 3 4 5 4

B D D B C B A G A B A G
↓ ↓ ↓ ↓ ↓ ↓ ↓ ↑ ↓ ↓ ↓ ↑
3 4 4 3 4 3 3 3 3 3 3 3

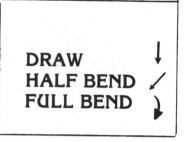

DRAW ↓
HALF BEND ╱
FULL BEND ↓

WILDWOOD FLOWER

B C D E G B C A B A G
↓ ↑ ↓ ↑ ↑ ↓ ↑ ↓ ↓ ↓ ↑
3 4 4 5 6 3 4 3 3 3 3

B C D E G B C A B A G
↓ ↑ ↓ ↑ ↑ ↓ ↑ ↓ ↓ ↓ ↑
3 4 4 5 6 3 4 3 3 3 3

D E B B A G D D E G E D
↓ ↑ ↓ ↓ ↓ ↑ ↓ ↓ ↑ ↑ ↑ ↓
4 5 7 7 6 6 4 4 5 6 5 4

B C D E G B C A B A G
↓ ↑ ↓ ↑ ↑ ↓ ↑ ↓ ↓ ↑ ↓
3 4 4 5 6 3 4 3 3 3 3

ON TOP OF OLD SMOKEY

G G B D G E C C D E D
↓ ↓ ↓ ↓ ↑ ↑ ↑ ↑ ↓ ↑ ↓
2 2 3 4 6 5 4 4 4 5 4

G G B D D A B C B A G
↓ ↓ ↓ ↓ ↓ ↓ ↓ ↑ ↓ ↓ ↑
2 2 3 4 4 3 3 4 3 3 3

GOOD NIGHT LADIES

B G D G B G A A
↓ ↑ ↓ ↓ ↓ ↑ ↓ ↓
3 3 1 2 3 3 3 3

B G C C C B B A A G
↓ ↑ ↑ ↑ ↑ ↓ ↓ ↓ ↓ ↑
3 3 4 4 4 3 3 3 3 3

Now you are playing your C harmonica in the key of G. This is known as cross-harp style, **blues** harp, or **draw** position.

All-time favorites you can play . . . .
Cross-Harp Style

Listen to the cassette tape while you are playing these songs.

MARY HAD A LITTLE LAMB

B A G A B B B A A A B D D
↓ ♪ ↑ ♪ ↓ ↓ ↓ ♪ ♪ ♪ ↓ ↓ ↓
3 3 3 3 3 3 3 3 3 3 3 4 4

B A G A B B B B A A B A G
↓ ♪ ↑ ♪ ↓ ↓ ↓ ↓ ♪ ♪ ↓ ♪ ↑
3 3 3 3 3 3 3 3 3 3 3 3 3

DRAW ↓
HALF BEND ╱
FULL BEND ↘

TWINKLE TWINKLE LITTLE STAR

G G D D E E D C C B B A A G D D C C B B A D D C C B B A
↓ ↓ ↓ ↓ ↑ ↑ ↓ ↑ ↑ ↓ ↓ ♪ ♪ ↑ ↓ ↓ ↑ ↑ ↓ ↓ ♪ ↓ ↓ ↑ ↑ ↓ ↓ ♪
2 2 4 4 5 5 4 4 3 3 3 3 3 4 4 4 3 3 3 3 3 4 4 4 3 3 3 3

G G D D E E D C C B B A A G
↓ ↓ ↓ ↓ ↑ ↑ ↓ ↑ ↑ ↓ ↓ ♪ ♪ ↑
2 2 4 4 5 5 4 4 3 3 3 3 3 3

FRERE JACQUES

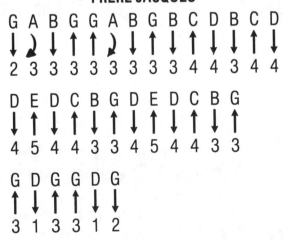

G A B G G A B G B C D B C D
↓ ♪ ↓ ↑ ↑ ♪ ↓ ↑ ↓ ↓ ↓ ↓ ↑ ↓
2 3 3 3 3 3 3 3 4 4 3 4 4

D E D C B G D E D C B G
↓ ↑ ↓ ↑ ↓ ↑ ↓ ↑ ↓ ↑ ↓ ↑
4 5 4 4 3 3 4 5 4 4 3 3

G D G G D G
↑ ↓ ↑ ↑ ↓ ↓
3 1 3 3 1 2

30

All-time favorites you can play . . . .

When necessary, STOP TAPE AND REWIND until you can play the song.
Then play the song without the tape.

LONDON BRIDGE

D	E	D	C	B	C	D	A	B	C	B	C	D
↓	↑	↓	↑	↓	↑	↓	↘	↓	↑	↓	↑	↓
4	5	4	4	3	4	4	3	3	4	3	4	4

D	E	D	C	B	C	D	A	D	B	G
↓	↑	↓	↑	↓	↑	↓	↘	↓	↓	↓
4	5	4	4	3	4	4	3	4	3	2

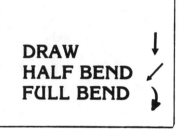

DRAW ↓
HALF BEND ↙
FULL BEND ↘

OLD MACDONALD HAD A FARM

G	G	G	D	E	E	D	B	B	A	A	G
↓	↓	↓	↑	↑	↓	↓	↓	↘	↘	↘	↑
2	2	2	1	2	2	1	3	3	3	3	3

D	G	G	G	D	E	E	D	B	B	A	A	G
↓	↓	↓	↓	↓	↑	↑	↓	↓	↓	↘	↘	↑
1	2	2	2	1	2	2	1	3	3	3	3	3

D	D	G	G	G	D	D	G	G	G	D	D	G	G	G
↓	↓	↑	↑	↑	↓	↓	↑	↑	↑	↓	↓	↑	↑	↑
1	1	3	3	3	1	1	3	3	3	1	1	3	3	3

D	D	G	G	G	G	G	D	E	E	D	B	B	A	A	G
↓	↓	↑	↑	↑	↓	↓	↓	↑	↑	↓	↓	↓	↘	↘	↓
1	1	3	3	3	2	2	1	2	2	1	3	3	3	3	3

FARMER IN THE DELL

D	G	G	G	G	G	A	B	B	B	B	B
↓	↓	↓	↓	↓	↓	↘	↓	↓	↓	↓	↓
1	2	2	2	2	2	3	3	3	3	3	3

D	D	E	D	B	G	A	B	B	A	A	G
↓	↓	↑	↓	↓	↓	↘	↓	↓	↘	↘	↓
4	4	5	4	3	2	3	3	3	3	3	2

31

All-time favorites you can play . . . .

Cross-Harp Style

Listen to the cassette tape while you are playing these songs.

ROW ROW ROW YOUR BOAT

G G G A B B A B C D
↓ ↓ ↓ ↘ ↓ ↓ ↘ ↓ ↑ ↓
2 2 2 3 3 3 3 3 4 4

G G G D D D B B B G G G D C B A G
↑ ↑ ↑ ↓ ↓ ↓ ↓ ↓ ↓ ↑ ↑ ↑ ↓ ↑ ↓ ↘ ↑
6 6 6 4 4 4 3 3 3 3 3 3 4 4 3 3 3

FOR HE'S A JOLLY GOOD FELLOW

D B B B A B C B B A A A G A B G
↓ ↓ ↓ ↘ ↓ ↓ ↑ ↓ ↓ ↘ ↘ ↘ ↑ ↘ ↓ ↓
4 3 3 3 3 3 4 3 3 3 3 3 3 3 3 2

A B B B A B C E E D D D C A G B
↘ ↓ ↓ ↓ ↘ ↓ ↑ ↑ ↑ ↓ ↓ ↓ ↑ ↘ ↑ ↓
3 3 3 3 3 3 4 5 5 4 4 4 4 3 3 3

D D D E E D C B B B C C B
↓ ↓ ↓ ↑ ↑ ↓ ↑ ↓ ↓ ↓ ↑ ↑ ↓
4 4 4 5 5 4 4 3 3 3 4 4 3

D B B B A B C E E D D D C A G
↓ ↓ ↓ ↘ ↘ ↓ ↑ ↑ ↑ ↓ ↓ ↓ ↑ ↘ ↓
4 3 3 3 3 3 4 5 5 4 4 4 4 3 2

WHEN THE SAINTS GO MARCHING IN

G B C D G B C D G B C D B G B A
↓ ↓ ↑ ↓ ↓ ↓ ↑ ↓ ↓ ↓ ↑ ↓ ↓ ↓ ↓ ↘
2 3 4 4 2 3 4 4 2 3 4 4 3 2 3 3

B B A G G B D D C C B C D B G A G
↓ ↓ ↘ ↓ ↓ ↓ ↓ ↓ ↑ ↑ ↓ ↑ ↓ ↓ ↓ ↘ ↑
3 3 3 3 3 3 4 4 4 4 3 4 4 3 2 3 3

32

All-time favorites you can play . . . .

Cross-Harp Style

TOM DOOLEY

D D D E G B B D D D E G A
↓ ↓ ↓ ↑ ↓ ↓ ↓ ↓ ↓ ↓ ↑ ↓ ♪
1 1 1 2 2 3 3 1 1 1 2 2 3

D D D E G A A A A B G E G
↓ ↓ ↓ ↑ ↓ ♪ ♪ ♪ ♪ ↓ ↑ ↑ ↑
1 1 1 2 2 3 3 3 3 3 3 2 3

DRAW	↓
HALF BEND	╱
FULL BEND	↘

SWANEE RIVER

B A G B A G G E G D B G A
↓ ♪ ↑ ↓ ↓ ♪ ↑ ↑ ↑ ↑ ↓ ↓ ♪
3 3 3 3 3 3 6 5 6 5 3 3 3

B A G B A G G E G D B G A A G
↓ ♪ ↑ ↓ ↓ ♪ ↑ ↑ ↑ ↑ ↓ ↓ ♪ ♪ ↑
3 3 3 3 3 3 6 5 6 5 4 3 3 3 3

O SUSANNA

G A B D D E D B G A B B B A G A
↑ ♪ ↓ ↓ ↓ ↑ ↓ ↓ ↓ ♪ ↓ ↓ ♪ ↓ ♪
3 3 3 4 4 5 4 3 2 3 3 3 3 3 3

G A B D D E D B G A B B B A A G
↓ ♪ ↓ ↓ ↓ ↓ ↑ ↓ ↓ ↓ ♪ ↓ ↓ ♪ ♪ ↑
2 3 3 4 4 5 4 3 2 3 3 3 3 3 3 3

C C E E E D D B G A
↑ ↑ ↑ ↑ ↑ ↓ ↓ ↓ ↓ ♪
4 4 5 5 5 4 4 3 2 3

G A B D D E D B G A B B B A A G
↓ ♪ ↓ ↓ ↓ ↑ ↑ ↓ ↑ ♪ ↓ ↓ ♪ ♪ ♪ ↑
2 3 3 4 4 5 4 3 3 3 3 3 3 3 3 3

All-time favorites you can play . . . .

Cross-Harp Style

WE WISH YOU A MERRY CHRISTMAS

D G G A G F# E E E A A B A G F# D
↓ ↓ ↘ ↑ ↘ ↓ ↑ ↑ ↑ ↘ ↓ ↓ ↓ ↓ ↘ ↓
1 2 2 3 3 2 2 2 2 3 3 3 3 2 2 1

D B B C B A G E D D E A F# G
↓ ↓ ↓ ↓ ↑ ↓ ↓ ↑ ↓ ↓ ↓ ↘ ↘ ↑
1 3 3 4 3 3 3 3 1 1 2 2 2 2

DRAW	↓
HALF BEND	↙
FULL BEND	↘

HOME ON THE RANGE

D D G A B G F# E C C C B C D G G G F# G A
↓ ↓ ↑ ↘ ↓ ↑ ↘ ↑ ↑ ↑ ↓ ↑ ↓ ↓ ↓ ↓ ↘ ↓ ↘
1 1 3 3 3 3 2 2 4 4 4 3 4 5 2 2 2 2 2 3

D D G A B G F# E C C C C B A G F# G A G
↓ ↓ ↘ ↓ ↓ ↑ ↘ ↑ ↑ ↑ ↑ ↑ ↓ ↘ ↑ ↘ ↓ ↘ ↑
1 1 2 3 3 3 2 2 4 4 4 4 3 3 3 2 3 3 2

D C B A B D D G G G F# G A D D G A B
↓ ↑ ↑ ↘ ↓ ↓ ↓ ↑ ↑ ↑ ↘ ↘ ↘ ↓ ↓ ↓ ↘ ↓
4 4 3 3 3 1 1 3 3 3 3 2 2 3 1 1 2 3 3

G F# E C C C C C B A G F# G A G
↑ ↘ ↑ ↑ ↑ ↑ ↑ ↑ ↓ ↘ ↘ ↘ ↓ ↓ ↓
3 2 2 4 4 4 4 4 3 3 3 2 2 3 3

THREE BLIND MICE

B A G B A G D C B D C B D G G F# E F# G D D
↓ ↘ ↑ ↓ ↘ ↑ ↓ ↑ ↓ ↓ ↑ ↓ ↓ ↑ ↑ ↘ ↑ ↘ ↓ ↓ ↓
3 3 3 3 3 3 4 4 3 4 4 3 1 3 3 2 2 2 2 1 1

D G G F# E F# G D D D D G G F# E F# G D D C B A G
↓ ↑ ↑ ↘ ↑ ↘ ↑ ↓ ↓ ↓ ↓ ↑ ↑ ↘ ↑ ↘ ↓ ↓ ↓ ↑ ↓ ↘ ↑
1 3 3 2 2 2 2 1 1 1 1 3 3 2 2 2 2 1 1 4 3 3 3

All-time favorites you can play . . . .
Cross-Harp Style

SHE'LL BE COMING AROUND THE MOUNTAIN

D E G G G E D D E G G A B B B B D B A G A
↓ ↑ ↑ ↑ ↑ ↑ ↓ ↓ ↑ ↑ ↑ ↘ ↓ ↓ ↓ ↓ ↓ ↓ ↘ ↑ ↘
1 2 3 3 3 2 1 1 2 3 3 3 3 3 3 3 4 3 3 3 3

D C B B B B A G F# E E E E A G F# E D D D D B A G F# G
↓ ↑ ↑ ↓ ↓ ↓ ↓ ↓ ↘ ↑ ↑ ↑ ↑ ↑ ↘ ↑ ↓ ↓ ↓ ↓ ↘ ↑ ↑ ↘ ↓
4 4 3 3 3 3 3 3 2 2 2 2 2 3 2 2 1 1 1 1 3 3 3 2 2

DECK THE HALLS

D C B A G A B G A B C A B A G F# G
↓ ↑ ↓ ↘ ↑ ↘ ↓ ↑ ↘ ↓ ↑ ↘ ↓ ↓ ↓ ↘ ↓
4 4 3 3 3 3 3 2 3 3 4 3 3 3 3 2 2

D C B A G A B G A B C A B A G F# G
↓ ↑ ↓ ↘ ↑ ↘ ↓ ↑ ↘ ↓ ↑ ↘ ↓ ↓ ↓ ↘ ↓
4 4 3 3 3 3 3 2 3 3 4 3 3 3 3 2 2

A B C A B C D A B C D E F# G F# E D
↘ ↓ ↑ ↘ ↓ ↑ ↓ ↘ ↓ ↑ ↓ ↑ ↘ ↘ ↘ ↓ ↓
3 3 4 3 3 4 4 3 3 4 4 2 2 2 2 2 1

D C B A G A B G E E E D C B A G
↓ ↑ ↓ ↘ ↑ ↘ ↓ ↓ ↑ ↑ ↑ ↑ ↓ ↓ ↘ ↑
4 4 3 3 3 3 3 2 5 5 5 4 4 3 3 3

RED RIVER VALLEY

D G B B B B A B A G D G B G B D C B A
↓ ↓ ↓ ↓ ↓ ↓ ↘ ↓ ↘ ↓ ↓ ↓ ↓ ↓ ↓ ↓ ↑ ↓ ↘
1 2 3 3 3 3 3 3 3 1 2 3 2 3 4 4 3 3

D C B B A G A B D C E E D F# G A B A G
↓ ↑ ↑ ↓ ↘ ↑ ↘ ↓ ↓ ↑ ↑ ↑ ↓ ↘ ↘ ↘ ↓ ↘ ↑
4 4 3 3 3 3 3 3 4 4 2 2 1 2 2 3 3 3 3

All-time favorites you can play....
Cross-Harp Style

AULD LANG SYNE

D G F# G B A G A B A G G B D E E D B B G A G B A G
↓ ↓ ↘ ↑ ↓ ↓ ↑ ↓ ↓ ↑ ↑ ↓ ↑ ↑ ↓ ↓ ↓ ↓ ↓ ↘ ↑ ↓ ↓ ↑
1 2 2 2 3 3 3 3 3 3 3 3 4 5 5 4 3 3 2 3 3 3 3 3

E E D G E D B B G A G A E D B B D E
↑ ↑ ↓ ↑ ↑ ↓ ↓ ↓ ↘ ↑ ↘ ↑ ↑ ↓ ↓ ↓ ↓ ↑
2 2 1 3 5 4 3 3 2 3 3 5 4 3 3 4 5

E D B B G A G A B A G E E D G
↑ ↓ ↓ ↓ ↘ ↑ ↓ ↘ ↓ ↑ ↑ ↑ ↑ ↑ ↑
5 4 3 3 2 3 3 3 3 3 3 2 2 1 3

JINGLE BELLS

D B A G D D D D B A G E E C B A F#
↓ ↓ ↘ ↑ ↓ ↓ ↓ ↓ ↓ ↘ ↑ ↑ ↑ ↑ ↓ ↘ ↘
1 3 3 3 1 1 1 1 3 3 2 2 4 3 3 2

D D C A B D B A G D D D B A G E
↓ ↓ ↑ ↘ ↓ ↓ ↓ ↘ ↑ ↓ ↓ ↓ ↓ ↘ ↑ ↑
4 4 4 3 3 1 3 3 3 1 1 1 3 3 2 2

E E C B A D D D D E D C A G
↑ ↑ ↑ ↓ ↘ ↓ ↓ ↓ ↓ ↓ ↓ ↓ ↘ ↑
2 2 4 3 3 4 4 4 4 5 4 4 3 3

B B B B B B B D G A B C C C C C B B B B B A A B A D
↓ ↓ ↓ ↓ ↓ ↓ ↓ ↓ ↑ ↘ ↑ ↑ ↑ ↑ ↑ ↑ ↓ ↓ ↓ ↓ ↓ ↘ ↘ ↓ ↘ ↓
3 3 3 3 3 3 3 4 3 3 3 4 4 4 4 4 3 3 3 3 3 3 3 3 3 4

B B B B B B B D G A B C C C C C B B B B B D D C A G
↓ ↓ ↓ ↓ ↓ ↓ ↓ ↓ ↑ ↘ ↑ ↑ ↑ ↑ ↑ ↑ ↓ ↓ ↓ ↓ ↓ ↓ ↓ ↓ ↘ ↑
3 3 3 3 3 3 3 4 3 3 3 4 4 4 4 4 3 3 3 3 4 4 4 3 3

All-time favorites you can play....

Cross-Harp Style

MY DARLING CLEMENTINE

THIS OLD MAN

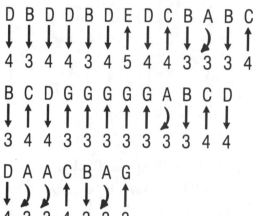

DRAW
HALF BEND
FULL BEND

O COME ALL YE FAITHFUL

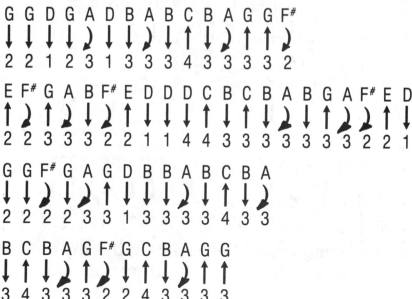

All-time favorites you can play . . . .

Cross-Harp Style

Listen to the cassette tape while you are playing these songs.

MOZART'S SONATA IN C

↓ ↓ ↓ ♪ ↓ ♪ ↑ ↑ ↓ ↓ ↑ ↓ ↓ ↓ ♪ ↓
2 3 4 2 2 3 3 5 4 6 4 4 4 3 3 3

↓ ↑ ♪ ↓ ♪ ↓ ↓ ↑ ↓ ↑ ↑ ↓ ♪ ↓ ♪ ↑ ↓
1 2 2 2 3 3 4 4 5 4 4 3 3 3 2 2 1

↑ ♪ ↓ ♪ ↓ ↓ ↑ ↓ ♪ ↓ ↑ ↑ ↓
2 2 2 3 3 4 4 3 3 3 2 2 1

↑ ↓ ↑ ♪ ↓ ♪ ↓ ↑ ↓ ♪ ↑ ♪ ↓ ↑ ↓ ↓ ↓ ♪ ↑
1 1 2 2 2 3 3 3 3 3 3 2 2 1 4 3 4 1 1 2 2 2

YANKEE DOODLE

G	G	A	B	G	B	A	D	G	G	A	B	G	F#
↓	↓	♪	↓	↓	↓	♪	↓	↓	↓	♪	↓	↓	♪
2	2	3	3	2	3	3	1	2	2	3	3	2	2

D	G	G	A	B	C	B	A	G	F#	D	E	F#	G	G
↓	↓	↓	♪	↓	↑	↓	♪	↓	♪	↓	↑	♪	↑	↑
1	2	2	3	3	4	3	3	2	2	1	2	2	3	3

E	F#	E	D	E	F#	G	D	E	D	C	B	D
↑	♪	↑	↓	↑	♪	↓	↓	↑	↑	↓	↓	↓
2	2	2	1	2	2	2	1	2	4	4	3	4

E	F#	E	D	E	F#	G	E	D	G	F#	A	G	G
↑	♪	↑	↓	↑	♪	↓	↑	↓	↓	♪	♪	↑	↑
2	2	2	1	2	2	2	1	2	2	3	3	3	3

Now you are playing your C harmonica in the key of G. This is known as cross-harp style, blues harp, or draw position.

Upper Register

So far we have learned to play the C scale of the middle register and the lower register. Now let's play the upper scale of the harmonica, holes 7, 8, 9, and 10. These four holes make a complete octave—C to C, one octave higher than holes 4 to 7. There is one note missing in the scale of the upper register, however, and that is B. This note is on *bend* BLOW hole 10 of the upper register. Look at the chart and you will see that the missing number is *bend* BLOW hole 10. B is the same note as DRAW holes 7 and 3—one octave lower.

Hole 10

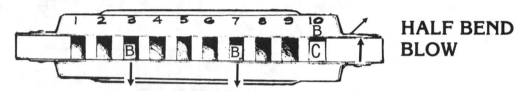

HALF BEND
BLOW

So we'll do some exercises together to get familiar with the upper register.

Start at hole 10 and count down to seven. BLOW all the notes as we did from holes 1 to 4. BLOW from hole 10 to hole 7. DRAW from hole 7 to 10, and then BLOW. Because the reeds are smaller, more air is needed, making it harder to play the upper register. Be sure to make an airtight seal with your mouth.

10	9	8	7		7	8	9	10		10	9	8	7		7	8	9	10
↑	↑	↑	↑		↓	↓	↓	↓		↓	↓	↓	↓		↑	↑	↑	↑

Now BLOW hole 7 as long as you can, and instead of taking a breath, DRAW as long as you can on hole 7. Repeat this step on holes 8, 9, and 10. Be sure you count the notes on the way up so you don't miss one.

FULL BEND
HALF BEND
BLOW

It is time to play the missing note B. In order to achieve this, we have to bend hole 10 as we BLOW. Remember, in "bending" the note, we alter it to produce the note one-half step lower.

The bend is in the *middle* of hole 10. To get all three notes on hole 10, it is necessary to DRAW to play A, bend to play B, and BLOW to play C. This completes the eight-note octave. **(See diagram 42D, page 42)**

Hole 6

BLOWING at hole 6 produces two separate notes. BLOW normally to produce G. Half bend to create the missing note B-flat. This note is difficult to bend and seldom used.

Many people are unable to play holes 6, 7 and 8 because they move the harp from their mouth or lose air pressure, causing an air leak.

Play hole 6, hole 7 and hole 8 back and forth five times.

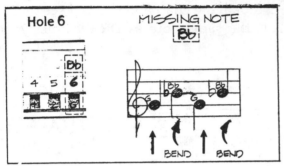 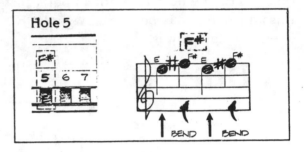

Hole 5

BLOW hole 5 produces two separate notes. Blow regularly to produce E. Half bend to create the missing note F-sharp.

The missing note, F-sharp in hole 5 (a half bend), can be found in hole 9 half bend and hole 2 half bend. Try to play 2, 5, 9, 5, 2. You'll need this F-sharp on hole 5 to play the diatonic scale in G on a key-of-C harmonica.

Hole 8

BLOW hole 8 produces two separate notes. BLOW regularly to produce E. Half bend to create E-flat.

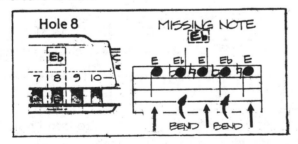 

Hole 7

BLOW hole 7 produces two separate notes. Blow regularly to produce C. Half bend to create B.

Hole 9

BLOW hole 9 produces three separate notes. Blow regularly to produce G, half bend to create one of the missing notes, F sharp. Full bend to create the other missing note, F. These two missing notes are very important.

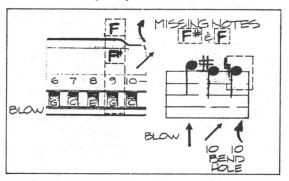

Learn these important exercises in the upper register.

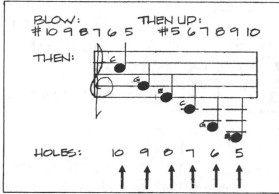

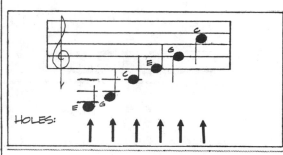

Just bend hole 10, hole 9, hole 8 and hole 7, it will take practice.

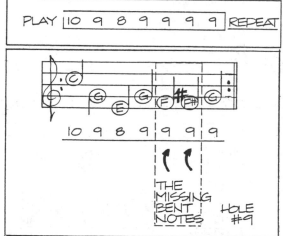

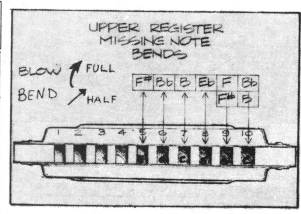

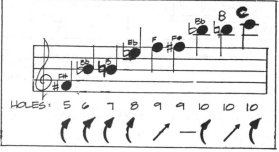

C HARMONICA

C HARMONICA LOWER REGISTER

	HOLE NO.		NOTE
BLOW ↑	1	C	DO
DRAW ↓	1	D	RE
BLOW ↑	2	E	MI
DRAW BEND ♪	2	F	FA
DRAW ↓	2	G	SOL
DRAW BEND ♪	3	A	LA
DRAW ↓	3	B	TI
BLOW ↑	4	C	DO

diagram 45A

C HARMONICA MIDDLE REGISTER

	HOLE NO.		NOTE
BLOW ↑	4	C	DO
DRAW ↓	4	D	RE
BLOW ↑	5	E	MI
DRAW ↓	5	F	FA
BLOW ↑	6	G	SOL
DRAW ↓	6	A	LA
DRAW ↓	7	B	TI
BLOW ↑	7	C	DO

diagram 45B

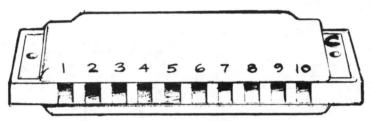

Harmonica is stamped "C."

C HARMONICA UPPER REGISTER

	HOLE NO.		NOTE
BLOW ↑	7	C	DO
DRAW ↓	8	D	RE
BLOW ↑	8	E	MI
DRAW ↓	9	F	FA
BLOW ↑	9	G	SOL
DRAW ↓	10	A	LA
DRAW BEND ♪	10	B	TI
BLOW ↑	10	C	DO

diagram 42C

HOW TO CHOOSE THE RIGHT HARMONICA

Harmonicas are manufactured in various keys. Use this chart to determine the key in which you wish to play:

TO PLAY IN THE KEY OF	STRAIGHT HARP 1st Position	CROSS HARP 2nd Position	3rd Position
F#	F#	B	E
F	F	Bb	Eb
E	E	A	D
Eb	Eb	Ab	Db
D	D	G	C
Db	Db	F#	B
C	C	F	Bb
B	B	E	A
Bb	Bb	Eb	Ab
A	A	D	G
Ab	Ab	Db	F#
G	G	C	F

The key of the harmonica is always stamped on the right side of the top coverplate. The highest pitched harmonica is in the key of F#, while the lowest is in the key of G. **diagram 42D**

Three Basic Positions (Approaches)

There are three basic approaches to playing the basic 10-hole diatonic harmonica. They are called *straight harp,* also known as "first position" (or blow position). *cross harp,* also known as "second position" (blues harp or draw position), and "third position." To simplify the matter, all this means is that with your harmonica you can play in three different keys, despite the fact that only one key is printed on the top plate.

1. STRAIGHT HARP (1st position or blow position) means that the piano, guitar, omnichord (or other chordal instrument) will play in the *same key* that is printed on your harp. (This is what you have just learned to play). For easy reference, the key note for this position is always located on the blow hole #1. This is your root note or home base. Straight harp is used for just about any style of music.

2. CROSS HARP (2nd position, blues or draw position) means that the chordal instruments will play in the same key as your draw hole 2. This is your home base (or root) note for this key. In other words, if the band says they are playing blues in G you use your C harmonica. Cross Harp is also often used for rock, funk, jazz, country, bluegrass, gospel, and some classical.

3. THIRD POSITION means that the other instruments will play in the same key as your draw hole 1. This is your home base (or root) note for this key. This position is used primarily for minor or "bluesy" tunes. It also can be used to get a jazzy sound. If the band is playing in the key of D-minor or a D blues you can use your C harp.

SUMMARY CHART OF THREE BASIC POSITIONS
(Using one harp for different keys)

Key	Position	Other Names	Home Base (or Root) Note Location	Music Styles
C	1st	Straight Harp Blow Position	Blow Hole 1	Folk, Country, Classical
G or G⁷	2nd	Blues Harp Draw Position Cross Harp (mixolydian mode)	Draw Hole 2	Rock, Funk, Country, Bluegrass, Gospel, Classical, Fusion Jazz
D or D Minor	3rd	None (dorian mode)	Draw Hole 1	Minor, Blues, Jazz, Rock, Funk, Fusion, Folk

(See diagram 42D, page 42)

Octave Location

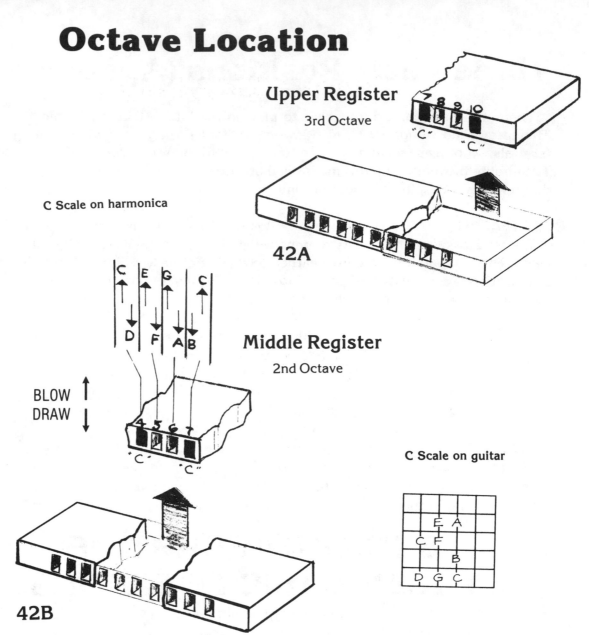

Upper Register

3rd Octave

C Scale on harmonica

42A

Middle Register

2nd Octave

BLOW ↑
DRAW ↓

C Scale on guitar

42B

Holes 1, 4, 7, 10 BLOW are all the same note:

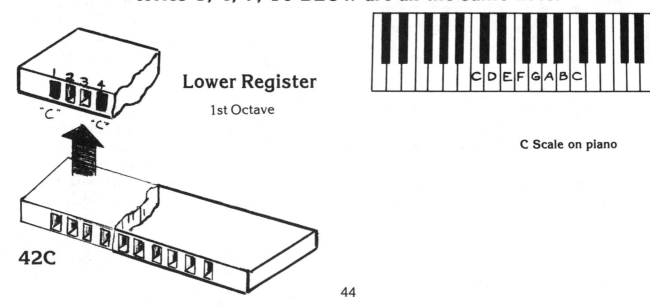

Lower Register

1st Octave

C Scale on piano

42C

44

Tongue Blocking

The technique of tongue blocking is very effective for self-accompaniment. It is also another way to get a single note without lipping and can be done while the tongue is left in the same position, either on the blow or draw.

Place your tongue over the first three holes so that air can only be directed into hole 4. When your tongue and mouth are in this position, it causes the chamber inside your mouth to become fuller, creating a clearer tone. It is a more brilliant, beautiful sound. In contrast, lipping is sharper in sound. Lipping is more appropriate for use in blues or country style.

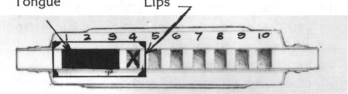

Tonguing is essential for playing the octaves. If no sound comes out, your tongue is probably covering all 4 holes. Study and practice.

Now we will practice some blocking techniques used in playing octaves.

Put your lips over holes 1, 2, 3 and 4. Go ahead and play all four notes at one time. Get a nice fat chord. Blow and draw.

Octaves

Tongue blocking is also used for playing octaves. For example, holes 1 and 4 are the same note only one octave apart.

When holes 2 and 3 are blocked, air flows through on both sides to holes 1 and 4 to make a complete octave.

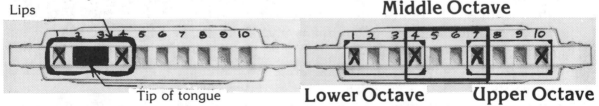

Now put your tongue over holes 2 and 3. Now play holes 1 and 4. You now have an octave, C to C. If you DRAW holes 1 and 4, it is D to D. If you are having troubles, play hole 1 and then hole 4, repeating this about ten times so that you can hear that 1 and 4 are the same note—one octave apart. Cover hole 2 and hole 3 and you will play an octave. Now BLOW hole 1, hole 4, hole 7, and hole 10. They are all the same notes, just an octave apart.

Try to play all the songs in Section I octave style and tongue style. This is a good way to practice.

If you put your tongue on hole 2 and hole 3, you will play the first octave, hole 1 and hole 4. Now put your tongue on hole 5 and hole 6 and you will play hole 4 and hole 7 on the sides of your mouth, which is the second octave. The third octave is in the upper register. Put your tongue on hole 8 and hole 9, and you will play holes 7 and 10.

BLOW hole 1 and hole 4; now DRAW. Play it easy (so it won't choke). Now blow and draw as long as you can. Now move up one hole and play hole 2 and hole 5. If you are having troubles with hole 2 and hole 5, try playing them "softer." Practice this experiment.

A hearty unique blend of chords can be achieved by blocking in various positions up and down the harmonica scale.

In the same "4-note" tongue position you can move up or down the scale sounding all four notes at once as you go. Experiment the length of the harmonica. But note that some of the chords will be discordant in the DRAW position. Some will be usable octaves on DRAW, and some will be blues chords.

Another unique effect can be achieved by moving the tongue on and off the holes while blowing and drawing. You won't always have a complete octave.

"Um-Pa-Pa"

One of the special effects you can achieve is the so-called "um-pa-pa" or the self-accompaniment effect. On the diatonic harmonica, the melody can be played in the hole at the right and the accompaniment or "um-pa-pa" can be attained by lifting the tongue up and down so that it alternately covers and releases holes.

Using this technique, "rhythm" chords are played on the *off* beat and controlled by a gentle flow of air from the diaphragm. It is an effect widely used in country music.

It is widely used in the tremelo *Echo* and so-called *octave tuned* harmonicas.

A wavering sound similar to vibrato can also be made by wagging the tongue back and forth. It is different from the sound made by the altering of the "chamber" created by the hands clasping the harp in that the sound waves are actually altered within the instrument to create tonal variations.

Now that you can play octaves, take a further step and play "um-pa-pa." A waltz is ideal for this style of playing. Start slowly and count to yourself "1-2-3, 1-2-3" and do it about 10 times to get the feel of this slow-flowing waltz music. Then BLOW on the harmonica, marking the beats with your tongue. Your tongue says "pa-pa." Put your tongue on holes 2 and 3, and play holes 1 and 4 to get the octave sound. Move the tip of your tongue on the harp on the "pa-pa's" (counts 2 and 3). BLOW as long as you can on the scale with "um-pa-pa"; then DRAW as long as you can "um-pa-pa." Repeat. Go up and down the scale with "um-pa-pa."

Now go back to Section I and play some of the all-time favorites in um-pa-pa style.

SECTION IV
USING YOUR HANDS

There are many ways to use your hands to achieve a variety of sounds and vibrations. Different speeds of opening and clasping your hands in such a way as to alter the "chamber" it creates generates such techniques as the "train," "trill," "vibrato," and "tremelo."

Every harp player plays in his or her own distinguished individual and unique way. You can say they are as individual as their thumbprints. One of the first things to practice when learning to play the harmonica is how to hold it.

How you hold your instrument will depend on the size and shape of your hand, the size and shape of your harmonica, and what is more comfortable for you.

If you are left-handed, it will probably be easier for you to follow all instructions the opposite of what is described. Be sure you hold the instrument so that the lower notes are at the left (like a piano keyboard). Blow into it to make sure it is not upside down.

This creates a perfect tone chamber.

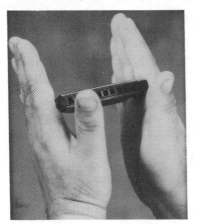
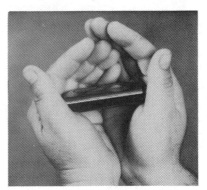

Leave your harmonica aside. Now go to the kitchen sink. Cup your hands and fill them with water. Right-hand fingers should overlap the left hand. Make sure no water can escape. If water comes out then adjust your hands. Hold water in your hands for thirty seconds without any of it spilling. When you can do this, you will have created the very kind of airtight tone chamber you need to generate the most advanced harmonica effects.

Once you've mastered the airtight chamber, put your cupped hands over your mouth to muffle the sound.

Use the outer edges of the thumbs and index finger to form a seal over your mouth. Then, with your cupped hands against your mouth, say into your hands "waawaa" for as long as you can.

Pick up your harmonica and create the airtight chamber so that the harp is inside. Now blow on any note. When you open your right hand—by straightening the fingers without "collapsing" the chamber—it changes the note from rich and resonant to mellow, in a very distinct and noticeable manner. Practice opening and closing the fingers of your right hand as you blow, to get the feel of the sound differences. Doing this fast creates an indispensable tremelo or vibrato effect. The tighter you hold your hands to your mouth, the fuller the sound will be.

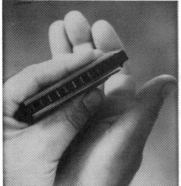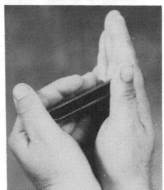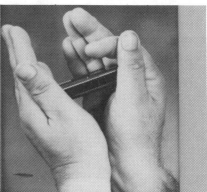

Some other ways to hold your harmonica.

Hand Vibrato

As we have seen opening and closing the right hand or flapping both hands will vary the sound. Do this as fast as you can then slow down as much as possible. Try to make your hands open and close with the rhythm or speed of the music.

If your hand is too small for these positions, try this variation. Place the harmonica between the thumb and index finger on each hand.

Half Cup

Hold the harp in your left hand and use your right to form a cup or a tone chamber between your hand and around the harp. This is called a *half cup*. The harmonica rests between the left hand thumb and two fingers. The edge of the right hand is placed at the bottom of the left palm like a hinge. Open and close your right hand in a pivoting motion to get the vibrato effect. Opening and closing produces the altered tone chamber. Vary the speed of the vibrato by changing the speed of the flutter in the right hand. Remember, the more tightly sealed your hands are, the better the effect will work. Try changing the speeds and noticing the effect.

Trill

Move your hands on the trill and not your head. Start with hole 4. Then drop down one note to hole 3 and play both notes one at a time back and forth as fast as possible. Try this on all the notes. The trill is playing two notes so fast at times it sounds like one note.

Start slowly and build speed until you can control sound. If you can't control it, back off. This exercise is good for the lung and the diaphragm.

Train

Another effect is the *train*. There are three ways to make a sound effect like a moving locomotive. Start by mouthing the words "chucka-chucka" on your harmonica without using your vocal cords. Take a short breath. Another sound effect is produced by making the "chucka-chucka" mouth motion by blowing and drawing on a single note as fast as you can. Create your own rhythm patterns. Start slowly and build speed until you can't go any faster while maintaining control. If you cannot control it, back off. this is good for the lungs and the diaphragm. Take two notes. Two blows and two draws are used to create the train sound. Blow and draw chords as fast as you can, but start slowly. Take two notes—preferably notes 2 and 3—and DRAW them two times—"ta-ta" somewhat fast and BLOW them two times.

Do this as many times as you can. If you practice this for one week, you will be able to change the rhythm to what you like, and it will sound like a train. It is useful for many other rhythm patterns.

Tremelo

To play tremelo, hold the harmonica in your left hand. Use the right-hand fingers, held together, to "fan" the air without moving the hand itself.

Throat Vibrato

Take a deep breath and BLOW into the harmonica, saying "oooooh" to yourself. Then draw and slowly say "ooooh, ooooh," with as many short breaths as possible. Tighten up your throat and bring the notes down to your diaphragm. Lodge your tongue in the back of your bottom teeth. Take short breath notes slowly for as long as you can. Gradually increase your speed until you are playing as fast as possible. Take short breaths, using your diaphragm. You are reshaping your throat muscles and diaphragm.

SECTION V
CARE FOR YOUR INSTRUMENT
Maintenance

Taking proper care of your harmonica prolongs its life and prevents damage such as air leaks and tonal losses. The harmonica is a precision musical instrument and should be treated like any fine precision tool. It is probably the most inexpensive precision tool made. The easiest way to insure long life for your harmonica is to keep it in its original box when not in use, and to avoid dirt, food and excessive saliva. Be careful not to drop it or cause any little nicks or dents which would interfere with the airtightness. Clean it regularly and properly. By following a few simple routines the instrument will stay in good condition. It will give you many years of enjoyment.

It's a good idea to rinse your mouth before each playing session to remove any trace of food or other foreign matter that can clog the reeds. Never eat candy or other foods while playing the harmonica. Any foreign particle, even a speck of dust, can lodge in a reed and cause it to stop vibrating or to vibrate off key. Avoid blowing too hard into the channels, too. This can damage the reeds by causing premature metal fatigue or misalignment.

After playing the instrument, always tap it sharply against the palm of the hand with the holes pointing down, to eliminate excessive moisture. Always wipe the playing surface with a lint-free cloth to prevent the metal from rusting.

Avoid excessive mouth wetness while playing to lessen the build up of saliva, which can deaden the reeds.

Heat isn't good for *any* harmonica, whether its base form is of wood or plastic. Excessive heat can warp wood easily, especially in the presence of moisture. Plastic has a higher tolerance to heat, but overexposure is still not recommended.

In extremely cold weather, avoid having the saliva freeze in your harmonica; it expands when frozen just like ordinary ice, and can warp virtually any material you're likely to encounter in a harmonica. Keep the harp next to your body where the temperature is not likely to drop below freezing. Warm the harmonica slowly when it has been exposed to an especially cold environment by blowing gently until it is up to ambient temperature.

Take care of your harmonicas.

Although the basic harmonica is a simple instrument its operation is more complex offering an infinite variety of tonal variations to the master player.

Sound is created by air passing over the brass reeds causing them to vibrate. The reeds are riveted over slots in the two brass plates attached to the comb. The slots are positioned over the channels where the air enters the instrument. The upper plate is positioned so that the slots are on top and the reeds underneath. It is activated by blowing into the channels. The lower plate is the same as the upper plate but its position is opposite, having the reeds on the outside. Sound is produced by drawing or blowing air through the channels. In a properly played and well fitted instrument air can only escape from the channels by passing over the ends of the free vibrating reeds thus producing sound.

When air enters the chamber it can only escape out of the reed slot, vibrating the reed and sound the note.

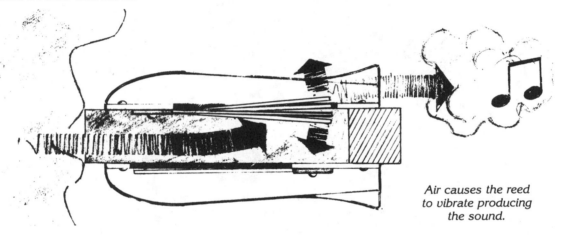

Air causes the reed to vibrate producing the sound.

I advise that you never let anyone else play your harmonica. There are two reasons for this. First, it is a very personal instrument, like a toothbrush. Common sense and good hygiene indicate the importance of keeping your own instrument free of contamination. The second reason is that every individual plays differently. Reeds that are "broken in" to your style can be blown out of tune by another player.

It is normal for harps to go out of tune and wear out, but with proper care an instrument can last a lifetime. The average life of an instrument for a professional can be years. For a beginner, the duration will vary, depending on how well it is cared for.

Dried saliva will build up around the openings of the air chambers. This should be removed by carefully picking it out with a sharp instrument.

For wood harmonicas some moisture is beneficial because it tends to swell the wood and improve the airtightness. Natural saliva is usually enough. The saliva works into every possible crevice and tends to swell the comb slightly. The saliva dries and forms a gasket-like matter which makes for better compression (like in a car). The notes can be more easily bent and the sounds are louder.

The Construction of a Harmonica

The harmonica is a finely tuned instrument designed to be easily held and manipulated by the hands and mouth. Traditional harmonicas are made with wooden channels or tone chambers, called "combs." The spaces between the channels are called "posts." Some newer model combs are made of plastic or steel. On each side of the comb is attached a thin brass plate containing the reeds. Both sides are protected by metal plates which are molded for easy mouth and hand use. They are usually held in place by screws or rivets.   This harmonica is shown to illustrate the position of the reeds.

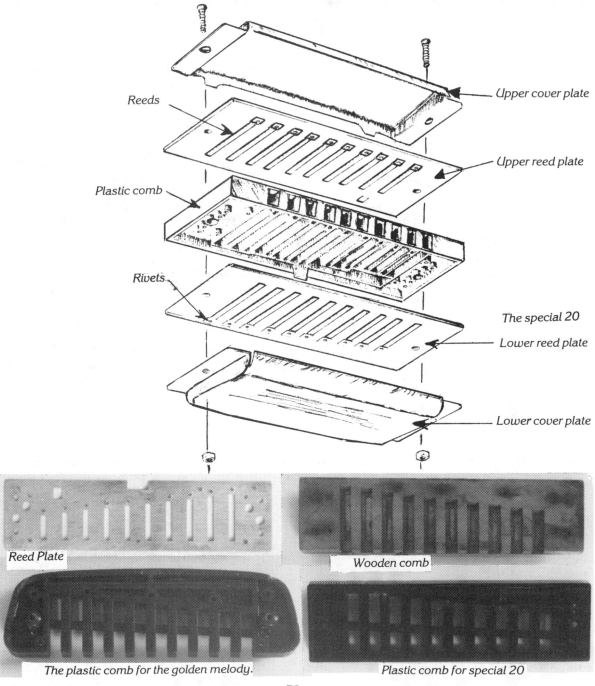

Upper cover plate

Reeds

Upper reed plate

Plastic comb

Rivets

The special 20

Lower reed plate

Lower cover plate

Reed Plate

Wooden comb

The plastic comb for the golden melody.

Plastic comb for special 20

The Reeds

The reeds vibrate freely in the channel. They are made of delicate, very thin brass. Every time the instrument is played the reeds vibrate back and forth at astonishing speeds. The upper A note on a C harp vibrates 880 times per second which is 52,800 times per minute.

Reeds are different lengths.

Overuse, improper blowing or just age can cause metal fatigue. This means that the reed eventually stretches out and vibrates too slowly, making the pitch sound flat. Sometimes the reed will bend to one side and come in touch with the reed slot, causing it to stop vibrating. Reeds do wear out and are replaceable. Sometimes they can be repaired by the user. However, it is wise to have repairs done by the manufacturer.

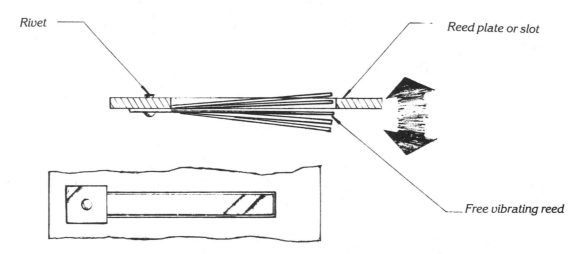

Rivet

Reed plate or slot

Free vibrating reed

The blow reeds are riveted at the top; the draw reeds at the bottom (see illustration of reed plates). The blues harp differs slightly from other types of harmonicas, because its reeds are raised slightly higher from the slotted brass plates, making it easier to bend the sound.

Upper reed plate (which is blow)   *Lower reed plate (which is draw)*

The standard harmonica has ten holes on each reed plate and can make considerably more than the obvious twenty notes most "campfire players" are familiar with. Each channel serves two reeds, a blow reed on top and a draw reed on the bottom. Ten reeds are riveted over the slots. They can be repaired and replaced by experts. Reeds are always made of a brass alloy because it is the only metal found that is capable of intense use, long durability, and the ability to bend sound.

For the harmonica to be played properly it must be completely airtight and free of any minute obstruction which would interfere with the vibrations of the reeds. Note control is lost if the instrument is damaged or poorly maintained.

Each reed is different in length and thickness. Air forced through the channels of the comb vibrates the unattached end of the reeds. The speed or frequency of the vibration produces the pitch. The shorter the reed, the faster it will vibrate and the higher the sound pitch. The longer reeds are heavier, vibrate slower, and have a lower pitch. The lowest sounds are made by reeds which are slightly weighted or thicker at the end.

Repairs

Harmonica repairs are relatively simple to make compared to other instruments. However, it takes much practice to repair your own instrument successfully. A beginner should never attempt to make repairs unless the instrument is so badly worn out there is little chance of ruining it.

Tuning

Reeds are tuned by filing with special tool or a fine jeweler's file. After the outside plates have been removed to expose the reeds, lift the reed to be tuned with the sharp edge of a razor blade.

To make a higher pitch remove tiny bits of metal by scratching gently with the tip of the file. Make a diagonal scratch in the metal near the free end of the reed. The more metal removed, the higher the pitch will be. To lower the pitch, make the diagonal scratches at the upper to middle part of the reed toward the end that is riveted.

It takes much practice to learn to tune the reeds properly and develop the "ear" for tone and pitch.

Sometimes a reed is blown out of balance so that it is not functioning directly over the open slot. Twisting the reed slightly with a pair of long-nosed pliers may free the reed. If not, you may need a jeweler's file to shave off the sides of the reed so it vibrates freely again.

Soaking

Sometimes the wood in a traditional model harmonica will dry out. This may be due to age, abuse, or excessive playing. Soaking makes the instrument more airtight. It also allows a stronger pressure of air that makes the reeds easier to bend.

There are several disadvantages to soaking and extreme caution must be used before any instrument is soaked. An instrument should be soaked only when it is totally useless in its present condition. In that case there are three options: throw it away, use it for spare parts, or soak it and hope it will be playable.

To soak, immerse it in warm water for a couple of minutes. Do not use other liquids because they may contain harmful chemicals that could destroy the delicate parts. Once a wood-combed harmonica has been soaked it must continue to be resoaked before each playing. Drying out causes the airtightness to disappear and worsens the condition. It can also make the painted surfaces peel and the wood comb warp or crack. It promotes corrosion in the metal plates and tends to damage the reeds.

After the instrument is soaked the wood will swell or raise above the level of the metal plates on the blowing surface. If this excess wood is not removed, it can injure your lip. Remove it carefully by filing with a fine file or emery board; or shave it carefully with a razor blade.

Remember that the manufacturer's warranty will not be accepted if the instrument has been soaked.

Selecting a Harmonica

There is a wide range of styles and models of harmonicas to choose from. There are only about half a dozen manufacturers in the world today but the Hohner Company is by far the largest manufacturer in the world.

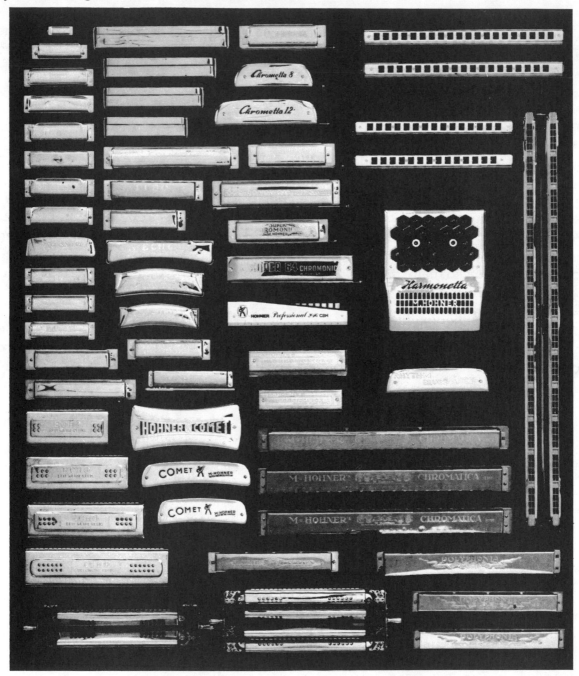

There are more than 50 types of harmonicas featured in the current Hohner catalog.

In selecting your harmonica it is important to consider what type of music you want to play, your degree of skill and the price you want to pay. More expensive models are made with higher quality materials and construction and are intended for the advanced player. Beginners should start with the less expensive model until they have mastered the art of blowing. These have less quality in the materials and construction, but are recommended because less will be lost by over-blowing.

Manufacturers warrant their instruments against factory defects. If there is a defect in a brand new instrument send it back to the factory with a short explanation and return address. Factory defects are repaired at no charge by most companies. Users are typically charged for any other damages.

There are specialized harmonicas for playing every type of music from blues to rock, country, jazz, folk and even classical. The octave-tuned double-holed harmonicas have a full-bodied sound with a strong tonal effect. The Autovalve harp is a double-holed harmonica. Chromatic harmonicas have sharps and flats with a twelve-note possibility achieved by a slide device, each hole having four reeds. Other popular models include the diatonically tuned Echo and Goliath harps.

There are a lot of things to consider here. If you're beginning, buy a Marine Band or blues harp. With blues harps, the reeds are slightly higher on the reed plate, so it's easier to bend the keys. The more professional harps are the "Special 20," "Golden Melody," and the "Master Class."

HARMONICA CLUBS

NATIONAL ORGANIZATION

S.P.A.H.
THE SOCIETY FOR THE PRESERVATION
& ADVANCEMENT OF THE HARMONICA
P.O. Box 865
Troy, MI 48099

REGIONAL CLUBS

BAY AREA HARMONICAS
1001 Woodside Ave.
Essexville, MI 48732

THE BIG HARP
P.O. Box 1211
Campbell, CA 95009

BLUE WATER HARMONICA CLUB
456 Little Ave.
Marine City, MI 48039

BUCKEYE STATE HARMONICA CLUB
436 Nashoba Ave.
Columbus, OH 43223

CAPITAL DISTRICT HARMONICA CLUB
1415 Western Ave.
Albany, NY 12203

CARDINAL STATE HARMONICA CLUB
219 D View Ave.
Norfolk, VA 23503

GARDEN STATE HARMONICA CLUB
P.O. Box 28
New Milford, NJ 07646

GRAND RAPIDS HARMONICA CLUB
7304 Edgewood
Jenison, MI 49428

HALTON HARMONICA CLUB
5349 Linbrook Rd.
Burlington, Ontario L7L-3T8 CANADA

HARMONICAS OF LOUISVILLE
325 East Southside Court
Louisville, KY

HARMONICAS OF MICHIGAN
2468 Somerset Blvd., Apt. 102
Troy, MI 48084

HOOSIER STATE HARMONICA CLUB
218 W. Main St.
Richmond, IN 47374

KANSAS CITY HARMONICATEERS HARMONICA CLUB
3024 North 47th St.
Kansas City, KS 66104

KANSAS HARMONICA ASSOCIATION
P.O. Box 1932
Hutchinson, KS 67501

LINCOLN PARK HARMONICA CLUB
1671 Mill St.
Lincoln Park, MI 48146

LONG ISLAND HARMONICA CLUB
P.O. Box 118
East Meadow, NY 11554

MAHONING VALLEY HARMONICA CLUB
581 Audrey Lane
Struthers, OH 44471

NATIONAL HARMONICA LEAGUE
182 Seafield Road
Bournemouth, ENGLAND BH6 5LJ

RUBBER CAPITAL HARMONICA CLUB
P.O. Box 53
Tallmadge, OH 44728

STEEL VALLEY HARMONICA CLUB
P.O. Box 3984
Youngstown, OH 44512

TWIN CITY HARMONICA SOCIETY
5031 Ewing Ave. N.
Minneapolis, MN 55429

VEHICLE CITY HARMONICA CLUB
3452 W. Francis Rd.
Clio, MI 48420

WYNMOOR HARMONICA CLUB
4301 Martinique Circle
Coconut Creek, FL 33066

FOR INFORMATION CONCERNING
THE S.P.A.H. CONVENTION,
WRITE TO:
S.P.A.H., INC., P.O. BOX 865,
Troy, MI 48099